D1554074

NAGASAKI

The Necessary Bomb?

NAGASAKI

The Necessary Bomb?

Joseph Laurance Marx

GAVILAN COLLEGE LIBRARY

The Macmillan Company / New York, New York

GAVILAN COLLEGE
LIBRARY

Copyright © 1971 by Joseph Laurance Marx

All rights reserved. No part of this book may be
reproduced or transmitted in any form or by any means,
electronic or mechanical, including photocopying, recording
or by any information storage and retrieval system,
without permission in writing from the Publisher.
The Macmillan Company
866 Third Avenue, New York, N.Y. 10022
Collier-Macmillan Canada Ltd., Toronto, Ontario
Library of Congress Catalog Card Number: 70-144819
First Printing
Printed in the United States of America

TO
R. P. M.

Contents

(Illustrations following page 116)

Preface

On August 6, 1945, a plane of the Army Air Force's 509th Composite Group, formed solely for that purpose, dropped the first atomic bomb. The target was Hiroshima. Three days later, the second atomic bomb was dropped on Nagasaki. Hiroshima brings instant identification, even to the young; yet people who were alive and conscious of events at the time have to be reminded of Nagasaki.

A resident of Nagasaki put it this way: it is terrible to live in a city that has been atom bombed, but worse that it be the second city so attacked.

The bombing of Hiroshima was the first most of the world knew of this fearsome new weapon. By the time word came of the second atomic bomb it was in some degree understood that a new force was loose in the world, a force to which it is still adjusting.

A couple of years ago I wrote a book, *Seven Hours to Zero*, about the bombing of Hiroshima. That book centered around the twelve men aboard the *Enola Gay* when it dropped the first atomic bomb—how and why these men were chosen and trained, what happened on that mission, what they thought of it at the time, what they thought of it now, and how it had affected their lives.

Writing about the Hiroshima bombing, I learned some things I hadn't known about the bombing of Nagasaki. Talking with people connected with both events, some questions were raised in my mind and I arrived at certain conclusions. Many months and more than a million words later, I decided my first conclusions were wrong. It is well known that it is easy to take a position on the basis of a few facts; sometimes when one learns more, he finds he must change his mind. I have changed mine.

NAGASAKI

The Necessary Bomb?

CHAPTER I

Special Bombing
Mission #16

At 0245, August 6, 1945, an overloaded B-29 (Superfortress) #82 with the name *Enola Gay* painted on her nose took off from runway A, North Field, on the island of Tinian in the Marianas, and headed northwest. At 1458, August 6, the aircraft returned, having turned around over Japan at 0915 to drop a bomb above the then almost-unknown city of Hiroshima.

At 0349, August 9, another overloaded B-29, #77, named *Bock's Car,* took off from the same place and also headed for Japan. Its target was the steel city of Kokura. Its weapon was a bulbous piece of metal known to some as Fat Man, consisting of a complicated detonating device, a number of electronic instruments and safeguards, and two small hemispheres of plutonium that together weighed only a few pounds but were capable of devastating a city.

Also on board *Bock's Car* were thirteen American servicemen, a full load of fuel, the usual complicated equipment of a big war plane, and some extra, secret equipment for this plane. By the time *Bock's Car* returned to Tinian, it would have used more fuel than it started with and left behind

1

its bomb, along with seventy-five thousand or more casualties.

All over the world, people intimately connected with these events were going about their business, most of them desperately concerned, most knowing nothing of what the others were doing. These were people with different political opinions, on opposite sides of the fence, separating Ally from enemy, men with such names as Truman, Stimson, Attlee, Stalin, Hirohito, Suzuki, Yonai, all working toward one goal—to get Japan out of the war.

Major Sweeney, the aircraft commander of *Bock's Car,* and the twelve other men aboard knew no more of the activities of these men than the statesmen knew of the thirteen, although some might have suspected what the men in the plane were about to do. Four days earlier, even fewer people, Japanese or Allied, would have suspected. Until August 6, the existence of the atomic bomb was the best-kept secret of the war. As of August 9, it was still not a fact known to most Japanese. Because of government censorship, not all the Japanese knew about it even after it had been used against them. Some of those who had heard about it believed it was more American propaganda, and most of those who had heard about it had no idea of its meaning. A large number of Japanese in Hiroshima knew, but they couldn't speak.

The Japanese government newscasts had euphemistically described it merely as a new-type bomb. President Truman, announcing it to the world after receiving word of its use at Hiroshima, pointed out that it was a use of the power of the sun. American planes had dropped leaflets by the thousands over the home islands describing what happened over Hiroshima. Despite this, the bulk of the Japanese people did not know about the terrifying possibilities of the new weapon. The regular bombs of the American planes were bad enough.

The men aboard *Bock's Car* knew—they had been the crew of *The Great Artiste,* the instrument plane on the Hiroshima mission. In addition to the regular crew, there was Lt. Jacob Beser, an electronics specialist who had had the same duties on the *Enola Gay* when the first bomb had been detonated. There were also two other men aboard who were not part of Major Sweeney's regular crew, Lt. Philip Barnes, listed as assistant weaponeer, who manned the "little black box" that electronically monitored the inner workings of the bomb, and Comdr. Frederick Ashworth, the "weaponeer" and man in charge of the bomb.

Three days before the *Enola Gay* took off, even those crew members who knew the power of the weapon were not using the word *atomic.* One of the myths that seems to persist about this event is that the crew did not know the nature of the huge, mysterious object it carried. During training it had been called a number of names: The Pumpkin, It, The Beast, or The Gimmick. Only those who had to, because of the nature of their work, knew what the bomb was. Many people did not; they could function just as well at their jobs knowing only a little.

But a few days before the first atomic mission, a small group of flyers, including the entire crew of the *Enola Gay,* attended a secret meeting in a Quonset hut where they were shown some pictures of the July 16 test detonation at Alamogordo, New Mexico, and given an explanation of what they were seeing. Not a total explanation; the word *atomic* was not used in general conversation until the plane was well on its way and it seemed almost certain that the bomb would be dropped in a few hours.

The news about the success of the Hiroshima mission reached President Truman aboard the destroyer *Augusta* as he was on his way home from the Potsdam Conference. He approved the immediate release of a previously prepared message describing the bomb to some extent, repeating some

portions of the July 26 Potsdam proclamation calling for
the unconditional surrender of all Japanese armed forces,
and threatening the empire otherwise with an unprecedented rain of ruin.

The Japanese government, and in particular the army,
did everything possible to keep word of this from reaching
the Japanese people. This secrecy or attempt at secrecy became very important as time went on and it became more
difficult to hide the truth.

At the beginning of August, 1945, Japan was thoroughly
beaten. The trouble was that most people did not know it.
A few Japanese knew, but even fewer were able to admit it
to themselves or to others. The United States did not know
it, nor did the other Allies. Japan had lost any chance of
winning the war a year or two earlier, and defeat was now
inevitable.

Arrayed on the other side were mighty war machines, including those of the United States, Britain, and the Soviet
Union, the first two only recently freed from the burden
of fighting a two-front war, the war in Europe having ended
three months earlier. America had developed the greatest
military manufacturing industry ever seen, one which was
still growing at the time. For the first time in the Pacific
war, manpower and matériel were or would be available in
almost unlimited quantities.

The only advantages the Japanese had were that the Allies
did not realize how desperate the Japanese situation was, and
the logistical edge of interior communications, an edge that
was daily becoming less important. The Japanese, however,
still had manpower reserve capable of causing tremendous
damage if they could be concentrated on defense of the
home islands. In what was now the far-off continent of Asia,
there was the formerly huge, still-feared, and almost-auton-
omous Kuantung Army. But the Japanese Navy was almost
literally nonexistent, and Japanese air power could not pro-

tect its few warships, or even the home islands. Worst was a fuel shortage which made impossible any wide use of what was left of naval and air power.

There was only one sensible solution for the Japanese: give up—surrender and make the best peace terms possible while there was still something to save. Some Allied diplomats and Oriental "experts" knew this; they couldn't see why there should be any attempt to continue the fighting, provided that their information and the hypotheses they created from their Intelligence were correct. But the difficulties of making peace for the Allied countries and in Japan were somewhat similar, though with one major difference. While any sign of weakness, any offering to compromise, might be politically dangerous for an Allied statesman, for a Japanese statesman, it would not only be politically dangerous but suicidal.

In all the events of human history, there is usually one opportunity where the course of events could have been changed and many lives saved. In the war between the United States and Japan, particularly during the last year or two, there were a number of occasions where the proper move by either country could have terminated the conflict and saved hundreds of thousands of lives. Unfortunately, however, the flow of events continued with the seeming inevitability of a Greek tragedy.

Moreover, each country misjudged and misinterpreted the other's intentions, actions, and motives. The Japanese consistently both overrated and underestimated the United States, and we made the same mistakes about them. Our knowledge of Japan and Japanese customs and manners of thought was slight, too much of it gained from such sources as *The Mikado* of Gilbert and Sullivan, J. P. Marquand's *Mr. Moto* series, or Puccini's *Madame Butterfly*.

A better understanding of the Japanese psyche might have helped avert war with the Japanese in the first place, though that is not likely. If the Japanese had fully comprehended America's power and character, they would never have attacked Pearl Harbor; if we had correctly estimated and known Japanese strength and weakness, we might well have taken different actions, both on the battlefield and on the diplomatic front.

There are a few words or concepts that cropped up repeatedly in my research and have a bearing on our story. The English word *polity* is defined as the form of government of a nation—its political essence. In Japanese, the word is *kokutai,* meaning national polity, ethos, customs, and way of life. Thus the Japanese word is broader in scope and laden with additional considerations.

Another word, *mokusatsu,* became important for a few days and almost prevented the Japanese from seeking a peaceful end to the war. *Mokusatsu*—derived from *moku,* meaning to be silent, and *satsu,* meaning to kill—can mean to ignore, take no notice of, treat with silent contempt, or all of these.

Finally, there is the word *haragei,* which is the technique of saying one thing and meaning another. This is derived from *hara,* meaning stomach, mind, intention, or spirit, and *gei,* meaning art or accomplishment. As is quite obvious, such a technique can make negotiation difficult, if not impossible.

Such problems were far from the minds of the men in *Bock's Car* as they flew through the night over the black Pacific. They were concerned with their mission, with what they would find when they arrived over their target, with whether they would meet with any fighter opposition or antiaircraft fire, with whether their fuel would hold out for the return trip, with whether the five-ton beast shackled in the bomb bay would perform as expected when loosed.

Lt. Jacob Beser, listed on the roster as ECM (electronic

counter measures), slept the sleep of the exhausted just as he had on the way to the target three nights earlier aboard the *Enola Gay*. Beser, whose actual reason for being on the mission was not known to most of the crew at the time, was there as a radar and radio expert. One of the bomb's fuse systems used radio beams bounced off the earth and timed. Beser's job was to make sure that the Japanese were not inadvertently using a wavelength close enough to those of the bomb to activate accidentally the bomb's radar fuses. The rest of the crew was also doing about the same things the other crew had done at the same stage of the mission. At this point there were only a few small differences. *Bock's Car* had a complement of thirteen; the *Enola Gay* had carried twelve men. While Colonel Tibbets had gone back to talk to the crew and tell those few who did not know that what they had on board was an atomic weapon, there was no need for Major Sweeney to do this. His crew had been along on *The Great Artiste* and had seen what had happened at Hiroshima; after that, restrictions had been lifted and the need for secrecy disappeared.

Major Sweeney had turned the plane over to the automatic pilot and to Capt. Charles Albury, copilot, and Lt. Fred Olivi, third pilot, while he caught forty winks to refresh himself for the coming work; many of the others napped, too, while their duties were light or non-existent. Commander Ashworth, the man in charge of the bomb, and Lieutenant Barnes watched the console, the "little black box."

Capt. Kermit "Tex" Beahan, the bombardier, dozed at times while mentally reviewing what Kokura, the primary target, would look like through his bombsight; M. Sgt. John Kuharek, the flight engineer, was busy, as he had been since takeoff, plotting fuel consumption and worrying; Capt. James Van Pelt, the navigator, kept track of their progress and course, occasionally checking his findings with S. Sgt.

Ed Buckley, the radarman; S. Sgt. Albert "Pappy" Dehart, the tail gunner, was at his accustomed lonely position in the gun turret and removed from everyone else except for communication by intercom. Sergeant Dehart's two machine guns were the only defensive weapons aboard the craft, the others having been removed along with other forms of protection, to save weight. Sgt. Raymond Gallagher, normally a waist gunner as well as scanner and assistant engineer, had only the latter two activities to stay awake for on the almost gunless ship, while Sgt. Abe Spitzer, the radio operator, had little to do at the moment, with no messages expected and radio silence being observed.

Around the world other people were behaving according to the demands of their natures and custom and the local times under which they operated. In Tokyo, Premier Suzuki slept the light sleep of the aged, his mind full of worries. In Moscow, Japanese Ambassador Naotake Sato had not yet recovered from the shock of a few hours before, when he'd heard Soviet Foreign Minister Molotov announce that the Soviet Union was now at war with Japan. In Washington, President Truman, Secretary of State Byrnes, and Secretary of War Stimson were wondering when Japan would announce its surrender and worrying about the future status of the Japanese Emperor. In Tokyo, a few young military officers were secretly making just-in-case plans for rash actions. Most of the people of the world who were interested knew something was up, but few knew just what, least of all the waking or sleeping population of Nagasaki.

As a matter of fact, few people in the world had realized the implications of the atomic bomb used at Hiroshima. From the time the success of the Manhattan Project seemed probable, the plan had been for two bombs to be dropped in quick succession. The bombs were different in make-up and method, but they were both atomic bombs using the power of nuclear fission, bombs of unprecedented destructive power.

The Hiroshima bomb was a uranium bomb, using the special characteristics of uranium 235, a refined fissionable version of the more common uranium 238. The bomb was conventionally shaped, but it was longer, thicker, and heavier than any previous bomb. Its method of detonation seemed simple. At the front end of the bomb was a cylindrical mass of uranium 235, by itself too small a quantity to be explosive. At the breech end was a pistonlike slug of uranium 235, similarly "innocent." Behind the latter was a small gunpowder charge. At the proper time that charge would be exploded, forcing one mass of fissionable material up the interior length of the bomb and inside the other mass, at which point, and instantaneously, all hell would break loose. The uranium masses, now combined into one, would become "critical" and start sending out neutrons in all directions, inevitably striking and releasing other neutrons in the surrounding fissionable material, creating a brief flash of heat reaching one hundred million degrees in a fraction of a millisecond.

The fissionable material in the Nagasaki bomb was composed of plutonium, a byproduct of uranium refining. Its method of detonation was completely different from that used in the Hiroshima bomb. Instead of putting two noncritical masses together to cause the detonation, one larger but still noncritical mass would be compressed to the point that it became critical. This meant the bomb was shaped completely differently. Instead of being long and tapering, "bomb-shaped," it was shorter, fatter, and more bulbous, more pear-shaped. Because someone, looking at mock-ups of the bombs, saw in them a resemblance to the tall Roosevelt and the chubby Churchill, they were called Thin Man and Fat Man for a time. The Thin Man, having been made smaller with improvements, became known as Little Boy after a time; the other remained Fat Man, or sometimes Fat Boy.

There had been no detonation of the uranium bomb before Hiroshima. The scientists were certain it would work. They were less sure of the method of detonating the plutonium bomb, whose fusing system was more complicated but whose end results were expected to be more efficient. Thus they gave the plutonium bomb a test run, the "Trinity" test at Alamogordo, New Mexico, July 16. Only after that successful detonation was the fissionable material rushed to the South Pacific for use in the war.

The uranium and plutonium reached Tinian two to three weeks before it was to be used in the two missions. Much of the radioactive material arrived after a record-breaking voyage on the cruiser *Indianapolis,* which set off for the Philippines after delivering its cargo, and was promptly sunk by a Japanese submarine. The balance of the fissionable material came by B-29 after a wild plane ride during which the craft had to turn back and land again in California. The almost immediate use of the uranium and plutonium was the result of one of the longest and most expensive military gambles ever taken.

Long before it was known whether an atomic bomb would work at all, much less *when* there would be enough of the then new and rare fissionable material to make it work, plans had to be made, installations built, people trained, planes modified; everything and everyone had to be in readiness at the right place and at the right time.

The 509th Composite Group had been formed and activated more than a year before to deliver on target a purely theoretical weapon whose manufacture cost two billion dollars. The 393d Bombardment Squadron, consisting of airmen and fifteen B-29s stripped of all armor and armament (except for the tail guns) and equipped with adjustable-pitch and reversible propellers and water-injection engines, had been training for the precise and new procedures to be used with an atomic bomb.

The people had been selected from all through the Air Force, and other Army and Navy rosters, along with technical civilian specialists. Most of the latter were scientists, engineers, and technicians working on the bomb itself at Los Alamos, Chicago, Oak Ridge, Hanford, and elsewhere, but a few of them were on Tinian, working on and supervising the final assembly of the bombs.

The whole organization was an anomaly in the usually strictly structured life of the armed forces. The 509th Composite Group was made up of less than two thousand men— someone once described the 509th as composed of 1,767 officers and men, a few civilian specialists, and Bill Laurence of *The New York Times*—and had been set up as an almost autonomous, self-sufficient group for only one purpose: to deliver atomic bombs on target. It was attached, loosely, to the global Twentieth Air Force; it operated in the Pacific Theater, whose land and naval forces were under the commands of General MacArthur and Admiral Nimitz. Neither of these powerful commanders had control over, or even official knowledge of, the new weapon until shortly before its use. In effect, through a unique chain of command, the 509th was responsible directly to the President of the United States. He was the one who had to say yes or no, do it or don't.

It was a most unusual group, the 509th. Rank wasn't as all-important as is usual in the military; each man of the entire complement knew he had been specially selected, but rarely did he know why. For the specialists on the plane that night, there was no question. Jake Beser, an electrical engineer from Johns Hopkins, had been taken aside shortly after joining the group and his duties explained; after that he was told, about the bomb, "Where it goes, you go." That is the reason he was the only man on *Bock's Car* that night who had also been aboard the *Enola Gay* seventy-two hours earlier. If there had been more atomic bombings, he would have been part of those missions, too.

Comdr. Frederick Ashworth, the man in charge of the bomb on this mission, was a weapons expert and a Navy man. His job was like that of Capt. William "Deak" Parsons on the Hiroshima mission, with one significant difference caused by the different methods used to detonate the two bombs. Both men were Navy in an Air Force setting, a little older than most of their coworkers, and extremely capable and popular.

A few days before the *Enola Gay* took off with Little Boy, Captain Parsons had decided to arm the bomb en route. Since it was detonated by a small powder blast sending one slug of uranium into another, he feared that an accident before being airborne might set off the gunpowder charge, starting a catastrophe that could blow North Field and most of Tinian off the map. Captain Parsons was Dr. J. Robert Oppenheimer's deputy, and Oppenheimer was the scientific director of the Manhattan Project that built the bomb. Commander Ashworth was Parsons's right-hand man, and like Parsons, had been in on the development of the bomb from the beginning. But because the plutonium bomb aboard *Bock's Car* was being made to be detonated by an implosion caused by the simultaneous setting off of sixty-three intricate lens molds that surrounded the plutonium mass, there was no way it could be armed while in the air as the Hiroshima bomb had been.

There were many similarities in the two missions, and a number of differences. One of the differences showed up in the atmosphere at the two aircrafts' takeoffs. When the *Enola Gay* had started for its trip, the field had been lighted up like an all-star movie's opening. The plane and crew had been surrounded by photographers who didn't know why they had been ordered to take all those pictures but took them anyway. When *Bock's Car* started for Japan three nights later, it seemed in many respects just another wartime flight. Not quite, of course.

For one thing, there were no other planes coming or going at North Field at the time, and special emergency crash teams were alerted and stationed at strategic points near but not alongside runway A. Another major difference was the lack of secrecy that had been such an important feature in everything that had gone before. When the *Enola Gay* had started, it was on its way to do something that had never been done, drop an atomic bomb on the enemy, a bomb that had never even been tested. *Bock's Car* was going to do a repeat job, and with a different type of bomb that had been tried out once.

But perfection can't be topped, or even repeated. The August 6 mission to Hiroshima had been, from a technical standpoint, perfect. After a fifteen-hundred-mile flight, the bomb had been detonated exactly on target, at precisely the calculated altitude, within seventeen seconds of the time planned for it.

For Major Sweeney and *Bock's Car* everything seemed to go wrong on Special Bombing Mission #16. For one thing, Major Sweeney and his crew were not flying their regular plane, *The Great Artiste,* which had been used as an instrument plane for the Hiroshima drop. Captain Bock and his crew were handling *The Great Artiste,* still fitted out as the instrument plane. Theoretically, there is no difference between two identical pieces of mechanical equipment, yet every machine has its own touch and feel. Just before take-off, it was discovered that an auxiliary fuel transfer pump wasn't operating properly, so that some six hundred gallons of fuel couldn't be taken from the reserve bomb-bay tanks and added to the regular supply when needed. This meant not only the loss of gallons of fuel, but the carrying of two tons of useless weight, cutting down on the plane's operating range in two ways.

Then, as the strike plane and the accompanying instrument and observation planes were taking off, there was another snafu that the crew of *Bock's Car* didn't even know about at the time. Dr. Robert Serber, a physicist, was to have been on the photograph plane, handling a special, high-speed movie camera. Some time after the three planes had taken off, he came walking disconsolately back to headquarters. He had been about to climb aboard when it was noticed that he had forgotten his parachute. Maj. Jim Hopkins, the aircraft commander, had sent him to get it; by the time he returned, the aircraft had gone. General Farrell, the Manhattan Project's ranking officer in the Marianas, decided to break radio silence, and after the two planes had reached cruising altitude, Dr. Serber, on Tinian, tried by radio to explain to Major Hopkins how the special camera operated.

Aboard *Bock's Car*, the main concern in the cockpit was the inability to use the reserve fuel in the bomb-bay tanks. But farther aft, Commander Ashworth and Lieutenant Barnes had a scare the rest of the crew wasn't aware of until it was over. All of a sudden, a red warning light on the "little black box" started flickering on and off in an irregular and alarming pattern. This could only mean that something was wrong with the intricate beast hanging in the bomb bay. The problem could have been anything from a minor flaw to a short circuit that could detonate a fuse and blow them all over the Pacific.

Theoretically this couldn't happen. The fusing device was complicated, with safeguards built in to prevent premature detonation. Three kinds of fuses were involved. The first was a timing device preventing the other fuses from working until a certain time had elapsed after the bomb had been dropped. That was to protect the plane and crew from being destroyed by a detonation too close to them. The second was a barometric device, making it impossible to activate the fuses until a certain atmospheric pressure was reached, one which was fairly close to the ground; the third was a, until recently, secret form of radio or radar fuse which depended on a radio impulse echoing from the earth. On the nineteenth bounce back, the fuse would be activated.

Now, for no reason at all that they could figure, an alarm light was flashing. Lieutenant Barnes sensibly started inspecting the wiring inside the monitoring box on the sound theory that it was at hand and that it was more probable that something had gone haywire inside the box than in the almost inaccessible interior of the bomb. Lieutenant Barnes started tracing the wires with his fingers until he came across two small rotary switches whose positions were in reverse order. The switches were quickly reversed, and the trouble light promptly stopped its heart-stopping flashing. Some time later, Commander Ashworth went forward to tell Major Sweeney of the incident.

At 0800 problems were continuing to arise for Major Sweeney and *Bock's Car*. They had flown over Iwo Jima, where a spare B-29 of the 509th was sitting on a hardstand to be used in case of necessity, and they had reached their assigned altitude of 31,000 feet over the rendezvous point, Yakashima Island, off the south coast of Kyushu, the farthest south and west of Japan's home islands. On schedule, the weather reports came in from the weather planes scouting the primary and secondary targets, Kokura and Nagasaki. The coded radio reports, of course, were not seemingly directed to *Bock's Car* but were merely routine reconnaissance reports being sent back to American headquarters, as far as the Japanese knew. Kokura was reported to be clear and cloudless and Nagasaki, hazy, two-tenths cloud coverage, clearing rapidly. Shortly after arriving over Yakashima, Fred Bock and *The Great Artiste* showed up.

But Major Hopkins and the observation plane didn't.

Instructions had been to rendezvous over Yakashima; if the instrument or photograph planes didn't show up, they should wait for them no longer than fifteen minutes and then proceed to target. The instrument plane had appeared within two minutes, but the photo plane was nowhere to be seen. Below, Major Sweeney could see two of the air–sea rescue planes lazily circling above two submarines also placed there for emergencies. But no Major Hopkins.

For three-quarters of an hour, Sweeney stayed over Yakashima, circling idly, using as little fuel as possible but still eating into the precious supply. With the imposition of radio silence, there was no way to call out, "Hoppy, we're here; where the hell are you?" After almost forty-five minutes, an annoyed Sweeney waggled *Bock's Car*'s wings to signal Captain Bock and turned northward toward Kokura, the "Pittsburgh of Japan."

Kokura was on the northern tip of Kyushu, about one hundred miles west-southwest of Hiroshima on the main island of Honshu. It had been chosen as the primary target for the second bomb because the big government arsenal there was a chief source of matériel used by the Japanese armed forces. Three other cities had been considered in addition: Nagasaki, an important port and manufacturing center on the southern tip of Kyushu, along with Niigata and Kyoto on Honshu. Kyoto had been dropped from the list, at the insistence of Secretary Stimson; being the chief shrine city of Japan, it had more cultural than military value. Niigata was scratched because it was too far from Tinian, being nearly five hundred miles northeast of Hiroshima. So Special Bombing Mission #16 had started out with only a primary and a secondary target.

While the people of Kokura and Nagasaki slept or went about their business with nothing to let them know they had been singled out for a special type of destruction, wheels were turning all over the world. Within the Japanese government, men of influence, power, and rank were vying with each other in their efforts to get Japan out of the war or to make sure there was no surrender. President Truman was wondering why there had been no satisfactory answer to the Allied peace proposals. Secretary of State Byrnes thought time was dragging by as he waited for word from the communications center and mentally ran through the options available to him.

The American and British military machines continued their build-ups of men and machinery for the great late fall amphibious assault on the beaches of southwestern Japan (Kyushu), to be followed by the spring, 1946, landings on the plains before Tokyo. Thousands of ships and planes and millions of men were being organized for the effort. Emergency hospitals were being constructed throughout the Pacific; and in Brookhaven, Long Island, New York, cinderblock housing was being prepared to care for the disturbed and shell-shocked survivors of the coming assault on the Japanese home islands.

What the Japanese began as a short-term gamble had turned into a seemingly endless nightmare.

CHAPTER II

The Long Bumpy Road
to War and Peace

It had taken an almost unprecedented series of mistakes, blunders, and miscalculations to get Japan and the United States into the positions in which they found themselves in the early 1940s. It wasn't, however, completely unprecedented: Almost all wars and confrontations are made up of blunders and miscalculations.

The military errors are easy to see in the clear view of hindsight. The Japanese military thought they could bring much of Asia under their sway, and for a time succeeded. When Japan first moved against Manchuria and then China itself in late 1931 and early 1932, she could possibly have been stopped by determined, concerted action on the part of the Chinese, British, and Americans, just as five years later, Hitler could have been kept from moving troops into the Rhineland. But the Chinese were disorganized and divided. Britain and America could not rattle the saber without taking the chance that it might have to be drawn, and no one in the West wanted a war at that time.

The United States thought that threatened economic sanctions and talk in the League of Nations, to which China protested, might do the trick without bloodshed—our blood, that is. The Japanese military machine got almost everything it wanted from the West, just as it had thought it would, and continued using the tactic of presenting the opposition with *faits accomplis*.

Japan had been a feudal, isolated island–state for centuries until opened to Western trade by Commodore Perry in 1853. This was followed by the abolition of the shogunate in 1867, the restoration of the Mikado, and the Meiji reforms to industrialize and modernize Japan. Feudalism was abolished in 1871, and a modern constitution promulgated in 1889. At various times after that, Japanese armed forces successfully moved against China and Imperial Russia, and in World War I, sided with the Allies, declaring war on Germany less than three weeks after the beginning of the war, thus gaining some former German Pacific territories after the war.

Japan had a long Samurai tradition, to which was added their unbroken string of successes in more modern wars. The Japanese saw themselves as unbeatable because of this warlike tradition—their will to fight and die before surrender. We saw the Japanese as small, clever imitators; they saw us as large, soft, and decadent, a people who would be unable to stand up to adversity or the spirit of a *banzai* charge.

Over a period of time, nations have come to regard other nations as being like themselves, thinking the same way, being only a little peculiar in speaking a different language, saluting a different flag, perhaps revering a different god. It seemed perfectly logical to Americans that the Japanese would be somewhat afraid of the larger, more mechanized Yanks. But to the Japanese, we rode, we didn't walk, and we would be no match for them in any kind of bitter, hand-to-hand fighting. Just because we were not Japanese.

For the fifty years before World War II, the Japanese

military had taken long risks and had won every time. They had trained class after class of devoted, service-minded young officers, who gradually rose in power and influence. They had combined the warlike Samurai influence with the mobility of modern methods of fighting, ending up with a large number of military men who actually believed that they were the only true patriots, the only real Japanese. Not all the Japanese military leaders fitted this pattern, of course, but enough of them did to make it seem to be a general trait.

The Imperial Army (and Navy and Air Force) came to be a government within the government, not only by habit and custom, but even, in a sense, by the constitution. No Japanese cabinet could exist without the Army's approval because the cabinet had to have a minister of war, and he had to be approved by the Army. Without a minister of war, no cabinet; no cabinet, no government.

The military had another weapon—assassination, or, just as important, fear of assassination. There were always some fanatical young officers who were sure they knew better than their elders, who were sure they were the only true, unselfish patriots, and who were only too anxious to take matters into their own hands for the greater glory of the Empire and the Emperor. When Japanese arms were successful, every move by a statesman or politician had to be weighed with this thought in mind. When things started going badly for the military, it was even more necessary for a politician to be careful, as the young officers were apt to be touchy and fretful.

We, in the United States, saw the Japanese government as a strong central structure, one that operated much the way ours did, because its form resembled ours in many ways. We had no idea that the Japanese State Department (Foreign Office) and War Department often operated on different wavelengths, that a Japanese statesman could make a remark that would be negated the next day or the next

week by the Army, even though the statesman could have
been telling the truth as he knew it at the time.

It is difficult for Americans to understand how the Japanese ever thought they could beat the United States in a
war. Nevertheless, the attack on Pearl Harbor was not the
rash act of a few people. It was a considered move by the
best military brains of the Empire and part of a long-range
plan. The plan was put into effect beginning with what
the Japanese refer to as the Manchurian "Incident" and the
later Chinese "Incident." It continued with the Japanese
takeover of various British and Dutch holdings in the
Pacific. Inevitably, it had to run head-on into conflict with
the United States.

The Japanese saw themselves as a determined, homogen-
ous nation of one hundred million people living on several
small, volcanic islands, being kept from their natural expansion and access to needed raw materials and markets by
a few powerful colonial powers. The Germans, in two wars,
likewise saw themselves hemmed in by unjust foreign powers
and wanted their "rightful" place in the sun and later
lebensraum. An earlier United States similarly displaced
Mexicans and Indians while driving westward toward its
"manifest destiny."

The Japanese plan was based on a three-phase development: offense, stabilization, and defense. The more hard-
headed military leaders, not so much a prey to their own
propaganda, knew that even the expanded Empire could
not compete in a materialistic way for long with American
power and resources. They figured that a quick surprise
attack could knock out the U.S. Pacific Fleet and give them
a couple of years to consolidate their gains, during which
time the American will to fight would be so lessened that the
United States would willingly listen to peace overtures and
compromises. And during that year or two that they would
have gained, the Japanese would be drawing on the raw

materials from their newly conquered areas, feeding them to the Home Islands, and getting back finished war material.

This was so much the basis of their strategy that the Japanese planning did not foresee a full wartime economy. As a matter of fact, Japanese war production peaked in 1941 and never approached that year's figures while the war was on. The Japanese planning included an America obsessed with its involvement with the Atlantic community and the Japanese use of Russia as a mediator between America and Japan. At the same time, Japan would have fairly well knocked out the British and Dutch as Pacific powers and would have been trying to mediate the war between Russia and Nazi Germany.

All these factors would undermine American fighting spirit. And besides, it was well known in Japan that morally and spiritually, no American could compete with a Japanese. Japan's strength lay in the spirit and sacrifice of her dedicated one hundred million; America's weakness lay in her decadence and lack of spirit, or so they thought.

For many months after Pearl Harbor, the daring Japanese militarists appeared to the Japanese people, and even to some of her more sophisticated leaders, to be right.

What these militarists did not count on was the quick recuperative powers of the American economic and military system. Within six months, though Japanese expansion seemed to be continuing unchecked, some Japanese observers could see that the tide was beginning to turn. Japanese troops had occupied huge areas, including the Philippines, but the May and June battles of the Coral Sea and Midway marked the end of the Imperial Navy's unchecked successes. Now, according to plan, should have been the time for phases two and three of the master plan, stabilization and defense.

It didn't work out that way. The United States, though undermanned in many respects, turned toward the offensive, and although some Japanese leaders could see that the war was going to be lost, none could afford to say so openly. However, Marquis Koichi Kido, the Lord Keeper of the Privy Seal, whose actual job was to be a private, well-informed adviser to the Emperor and constantly in attendance on him, saw the handwriting on the wall. He suggested to the Emperor that it would be a good idea to negotiate for peace at that time. Since Singapore was about to fall to the Imperial Army, this was a rather startling suggestion. A little later, Kido received word from Ambassador Mamoru Shigemitsu, returning from China, that the situation there was not nearly as rosy as the Japanese Army was saying. Shigemitsu suggested a change in policy that would recognize Chinese sovereignty and independence. For some reason, the military did not take kindly to this notion, when informally approached, and nothing came of it. When Shigemitsu became Foreign Minister, in 1943, he began to work to set into action a new China policy.

A rather confusing series of events followed, events that came to nothing but had interesting implications. The Chiang Kai-shek government in China, through intermediaries, suggested a way to negotiate a settlement of the Sino–Japanese problem. As it was presented to the Japanese, Chiang wanted to stop cooperating with the Chinese Communists so that he could fight them and hopefully bring them, or many of them, into his camp. To do this, he would have to stop fighting the Japanese. He proposed that if Japan would withdraw its troops from China, he might think about severing relations with the Western military powers.

The Japanese didn't say yes or no; they were not at all sure of the validity of the offer, although much of it was delivered personally in Tokyo by a high official in the Nanking government, supposedly at the request of the government in Chungking. Japan's Premier Tojo suggested that the possible peace talks take place, but stated that Japan would take no official part in them at the moment. He said, however, that if Chiang severed relations with the United States and Britain, then the Japanese might consider withdrawing her troops from China.

Marquis Kido and Shigemitsu were not the only ones who could see and read the handwriting on the wall. A Japanese admiral came to the same conclusion on the basis of facts he was able to dig up while conducting his own secret work. He was Rear Adm. Sokichi Tagaki, attached to the ministerial secretariat of the naval general staff. As such, he was primarily a research man. Navy Minister Shimada set him to work on a secret assignment: to study the lessons of the war to date. Because by this time the Imperial Navy (and Army) were beginning to lose battles and positions, as well as men and ships and land, and a good department tries to find out why, so future errors may be avoided.

Tagaki did his work well; a capable and conscientious researcher, he had enough independence of mind to see where the facts were leading him, even if he didn't like what he saw. His research showed him, quite clearly, that Japan was in the process of losing the war, that Japan *would* lose the war because there was no way she could win. Therefore, as a patriotic and logical man, he drew the next conclusion: Japan would have to find a way for a compromise peace.

Granted that Admiral Tagaki was a patriotic and intelligent man, that did not mean he wanted to be a former admiral or a dead patriot. The Navy Minister was a close friend and henchman of Premier Tojo. According to Tagaki's findings, Tojo would be joining the list of former premiers and Tojo's friend Shimada would be out with him. Tagaki would be considered a traitor by the young officers and would be liquidated. This would not do anyone any good, because his findings would never become known to those who ought to know them and do something about them.

The facts were, to Takagi, conclusive. He could put together the Empire's losses, the replacements, the current and recent rate of loss and replacement, and see nothing but a rapid road downhill. But if he made his report public, that is, turned it in with its defeatist conclusions to his superiors, it would never see the light of day, and he might not see too many days himself. Consequently, he did what seemed to him to be the wisest and most prudent thing— he kept his findings to himself. He planned to let his findings drop, little by little, a few points at a time, to a few key men he could trust, men who had views like his own on the war. In March, 1944, four months before Tojo's fall from power, Sokichi Takagi told Admirals Yonai and Inouye of his conclusions, telling them in person, not in the form of the usual written memo. They listened. No overt action was taken.

Even high military officers could get into trouble from writing papers others considered unpatriotic. Col. Makoto Matsutani, along with a group of general staff officers handling war plans, circulated a document to the top Army and Navy brass. The plans officers were concerned about the actions Japan should take after Germany's collapse in Europe, which they could see coming, and which included several alternatives, trying to save what they could. The last alternative was what action to take should it become a question of national suicide or total surrender. The conclusion was that in this event, Japan would have to surrender with nothing more than an Allied promise to preserve the homeland and national polity. Although not one of the men who saw the plans raised any objections, after Colonel Matsutani had explained them to Premier Tojo, the colonel was abruptly reassigned to duty in China.

There were a good many in Japan who could see the shape of the future. But they couldn't admit it in public, some of them found it difficult even to admit it to themselves. The dangerous web woven in deceit can trap the weavers. For years now the military had been running the government. Not officially, but unmistakably, they were the masters. They had let the Japanese people know only what they, the masters, thought was good for them. The people had been fed on lies, they had been told only of victories, there had been no defeats. Now, how could they be told that the Empire of the Rising Sun, a swollen Colossus bestriding the Pacific, was a balloon that had been blown up out of all shape?

Even the Emperor, divine being that he was, couldn't say aloud what he privately knew. If by any chance, the Emperor said or did anything the military didn't approve of, it was, they explained, because he had been misled by his weak, traitorous advisers. The military had had its own way for so long that it took its right to rule for granted. Being made up of men, it made mistakes. But these men, unlike most other men, could not admit to these mistakes without breaching the foundations of their own edifice. So, as the Japanese Empire grew smaller, as her hold on vast reaches of the Pacific grew more and more tenuous, the people at home were told only of victories or minor withdrawals. When there were no more victories to be celebrated and it was becoming too difficult to invent them, someone had to pay. In the immemorial manner of politics, the government had to fall.

The Japanese have an institution called the *jushin*. Membership is limited to elder statesmen who have at some time been premiers. That was about all they had in common. In today's language, some were conservative, some comparatively liberal, some hawks, some doves. They were impressive in years and names, but except for the weight of their ages and reputations, they had no real power.

Nevertheless, they decided they should take some action. They, too, could see that Germany was going to lose in Europe, that Japan would be fighting alone in the Pacific, and that they were already losing, which meant that Tojo's government would inevitably topple. At one point, the *jushin,* trying to bore from within, wanted to get one of their number, Adm. Mitsumasa Yonai into the Tojo cabinet. Yonai had been premier in 1940. He had lost his position at that time as he had been against the alliance with Germany and Italy and sometimes critical of going to war against America. Tojo would not make him Navy Minister, so the idea of having one of their men in the cabinet was dropped.

A little later, the *jushin,* concerned over the conduct of the war, advised some changes. Tojo accused them of attempting to overthrow his cabinet. A year later, with the fall of Saipan and the situation deteriorating all around, they did just that. Taking advantage of Tojo's domestic unpopularity, the *jushin* adopted a resolution that said nothing about losing the war but mentioned the difficulties the nation was in and suggested a strong new national cabinet. Tojo countered in the manner any desperate politician would: He offered to cooperate with the elder statesmen, giving them official advisory status and offering two of them, including Yonai, places in a new cabinet. He was too late. His government fell.

It was replaced in July, 1944, by what turned out to be an interim cabinet, an odd sort of two-headed governing body, consisting of Gen. Kuniaki Koiso and Admiral Yonai, with Koiso officially the premier and Yonai as copremier and Navy Minister. The reasons for this were desperation and distrust—a dilemma that plagued Japan for some time.

The *jushin* were disenchanted with the military who had run the country with a strong hand for too long. On the other hand, the country was at war and the military was still strong, so a purely civilian premier would not be acceptable to them, unless it was someone of overwhelming stature. The *jushin* suggested three names: Generals Koiso, Terauchi, and Hata. Tojo, though on his way out, still had a voice. He ruled out Terauchi, a man with whom he did not get along. Hata, a field marshal, was head of the Second Army, with headquarters at Hiroshima, and while the senior statesmen wanted a man with military know-how, they did not want to appoint an active high-ranking general whose absence from the field might weaken the military power as well as be bad for the morale of the Army.

Complicating the issue was the feeling of some of the *jushin* that almost as great a danger as the rigid thinking of the regular military was the small but organized Communist element in the Army. While Admiral Yonai privately pointed out the dangers of putting into office traditional military men with their one-sided education and outlook, other high-ranking officials were equally afraid that a non-military man could not get the Army's backing or be able to hold off the extreme left-wing element in the armed forces. So Koiso, a retired general serving as governor of Korea, was chosen as a compromise. However, because the *jushin* was not too sure of his views and reactions, a two-headed beast was devised, with Admiral Yonai in the yoke as copremier.

The basic purpose of the Koiso cabinet was to be a transitional "peace" cabinet. Koiso evidently didn't realize this. When he was given the appointment by the Emperor, all he was told, in the usually old-fashioned and stilted court language, was that the cabinet was being formed to attain the objectives of the Greater East Asia War, which by this time included the destruction of American and British power in the area.

Events during the period of Koiso's reign would have been difficult for anyone, and Koiso, from his record, was not the most astute politician. He took over at a time when Japanese forces were losing every battle and he did not improve matters with several of his rash statements. Nor was he helped by the fact that he often did not know what the military was doing or planning. He made efforts to be filled in on military plans and was rebuffed.

With Yonai as Navy Minister, Admiral Tagaki returned to the General Staff, and again he was given a secret assignment. He was to make a survey of the problems of easing Japan out of the war without doing too much damage to her self-esteem. This problem was divided into two parts: Could any government get the Army to agree to ending the war on any basis except the impossible one of victory? How could an end of the war without victory be presented to the population as a whole?

The answers to both questions were the same. The only way that could be foreseen for the armed forces to lay down their arms would be on orders from the Emperor, and the only person who could "sell" the general public on the desirability of ending the war without victory was the same man.

But even for this revered figure, the way had to be prepared if he was to be effective. This brings up another American misconception about Japan: the position of the Emperor. For a number of reasons, including *The Mikado* and propaganda from both sides, we had considered the Japanese Emperor as being an all-powerful monarch. Despite warnings from people who knew better, most Americans continued to regard him that way until long after the war was over. Actually, the Emperor of Japan is much more

of a religious figure and symbol than a man with great
temporal power.

Conditions in Japan were going from bad to worse at a
breakneck pace. For some time the Army and Navy had
been taking a beating on almost all fronts; now it was time
for the people at home to share the burden. Soon after
October, 1944, when the Navy ceased to exist as a functioning offensive entity because of heavy losses in the Philippines, island-based B-29s started regular mass attacks on the
homeland. Bit by bit, city by city, they were pulverizing
Japan's industries and urban concentrations.

Koiso's downfall was triggered by the Philippines campaign and was hastened immeasurably by a double-cross by
the military—or perhaps it would be kinder to say by a lack
of trustworthy communications with the military. At the
beginning of the Leyte campaign, the Supreme Command
let the premier know that this was going to be perhaps the
decisive battle of the war. The Americans were making an
all-out effort to recapture Leyte; the Japanese would make
their stand there and repel them. Koiso repeated this to
the Japanese people. A few days before the United States
announced the successful conclusion of its Leyte operation,
the Japanese War Minister told Koiso that the Supreme
Command had changed its mind, that the decisive stand
would be taken on Luzon, not Leyte.

By January, 1945, the Emperor knew he must see that
Japan had a government that could get the country out of
the war and ensure a certain amount of postwar stability. To
that end, he thought it might be a good idea if the *jushin*
were gathered together to advise the Emperor on the war
situation. Marquis Kido thought that this would probably
provoke the military, at least one of whom, Tojo, as a
former premier, would see it as an attempt by the politicians
to circumvent the military. Marquis Kido suggested that

the Emperor see the elder statesmen individually on different days.

The *jushin,* composed of men who had led their country, could hardly be called stupid. But at these meetings the individuals either didn't know or didn't say what the Emperor wanted to hear: that the situation was hopeless, that he should act, and that they'd be glad to help if they could. Instead, different men spoke about the deteriorating food situation, Russian–American relations, and other fascinating and important subjects, germane, but skipping the central issue. We've lost the war, how are we going to get out of it with, if not a whole skin, at least a little covering?

There was one man who spoke out, Prince Konoye, long a favorite of the Emperor. Konoye started out with the premise that Japan had already lost the war. He felt that British and American feeling had not hardened to the point that a complete change in Japan's polity would be a prerequisite for peace. Then he expounded on his *bête noire,* the danger of communism, the local variety and that borrowed from Russia, a country he saw just waiting to swing down and swallow Japan, either from without or with help from within.

These February meetings with the Emperor produced a large amount of talk and no action. Two separate "peace balloons" were shot down—in actuality they never got off the ground. One was another doubtful Chinese effort, offering about the same terms as the previous one; the other was an attempt to use the good offices of Sweden. In the back of the minds of many Japanese leaders was the possibility of using the Soviet Union, especially considering Japan's unique position vis-à-vis Germany and Russia. Japan, an ally of Germany, was also bound by a treaty of friendship and neutrality with Russia.

The Japanese had hopes of using their position to break

D
767.25
N3
M35

Marx, Joseph
Nagasaki : the
necessary bomb?

40850

GAVILAN COLLEGE
LIBRARY

up the war between its ally Germany and its "friend." Japan also hoped to use her position to have Russia be the intermediary between the island empire and Britain and the United States. For a number of reasons, all these were false hopes, based on wishes rather than reality.

Meanwhile, the war in Europe was drawing to a close as Soviet and British–American forces closed in on Germany. And in the Pacific, Allied troops landed in strength on Okinawa (April 1, 1945) beginning the last big land battle of the war. Almost immediately after that, the Soviet government announced in Moscow that it was not going to renew the neutrality pact with Japan, which was supposed to run until April, 1946. The Japanese thought this gave them another year of grace in which they could get out of the war.

The Koiso cabinet, however, had only a few days of grace. The series of defeats, along with the lack of harmony on the home front, was too much. Premier Koiso advised Marquis Kido that he could not continue, primarily because of the differences between the government and the Supreme Command. Koiso suggested that an Imperial Headquarters cabinet be formed so that the political heads of the government could participate directly in the conduct of the war. Marquis Kido took this up with the Ministers of War and Navy and was turned down, immediately and flatly. The military wouldn't stand for any interference from civilians. So, once again, the ball was tossed back to the *jushin*.

These elder statesmen had the same old problem. Who could be trusted to run a "peace" cabinet and also have the confidence of the military?

For a number of reasons, an old man, Adm. Baron Kantaro Suzuki, retired, was chosen to be the last wartime premier. Suzuki was no politician, which added to his attractiveness for the post. He was seventy-seven, a hero of the 1904–1905 Russo–Japanese War, when as a young naval officer he had led the decisive attack against the ill-fated Russian Baltic Fleet at Tsushima. Suzuki, when he became premier, was quite deaf, probably senile, a heavy drinker and smoker, and a man who changed his mind as often as a capricious woman. He was also revered as a hero, definitely liked as a person, and had an almost obsessive and well-founded fear of assassination.

Kantaro Suzuki was, for a time, all things to all men. At least to all the men who counted in Japan at the time. To the military hard-liners, he was a true patriot, cast in the old heroic mold, and what's more, he was no politician. To those who wanted a quick end to the war, he was a revered figure who was not tied down by the strait jacket of military thinking.

The tip-off to Suzuki's thinking came when he formed his cabinet and had to choose a foreign minister. He was considering three men. Togo, Shigemitsu, and Hirota. All three had, at one time or another, been Japanese ambassadors to Moscow. Shigemitsu, Foreign Minister in the Koiso cabinet, would have seemed a natural, but the outgoing Koiso reportedly didn't want to see his former minister reappointed by his successor. When former Premier Koki Hirota was sounded out, he suggested Shigenori Togo, who had been Foreign Minister in Tojo's cabinet at the beginning of the war. He had disagreed fairly consistently with Premier Tojo and had finally resigned September 1, 1942.

From the point of view of the well-informed Japanese, Togo was a "peace" man. To the United States, he was simply the man who had been Foreign Minister at the time of Pearl Harbor and therefore a man not to be trusted. Actually, when called out of retirement to take back his old post, Togo refused until he had assured himself that Suzuki had every intention of ending the war on any terms possible.

At this time in Japanese history, when its leaders were

divided on the issue of prosecuting the war with full vigor
or asking for peace, Suzuki may have been the ideal premier.
He was esteemed as a wise and brave man, but he seemed
to have trouble making up his mind and sticking to it. He
was a master of the Japanese art of *haragei,* which means, in
effect, the practice of saying one thing and meaning another.
Although this is an art that isn't unusual in the arsenal of
a politician's weapons, Suzuki wasn't supposed to be a politician. Be that as it may, from the time the old sea dog
became premier, it was impossible to figure out what he
was going to do from what he said. In this way, he confused
both friend and foe, backer and enemy. Evidently, he did
not confuse the Emperor, who could not conceive of the
old man doing anything that wasn't completely loyal and
honorable.

The long list of public statements about fighting to the
last man and private remarks about the need for seeking
a peace before the nation was destroyed could lead to nothing but more confusion. The most polite thing to say is
that this was an example of using *haragei* to gain desirable
ends without being assassinated in the process. This fear of
assassination recurs time and again, with good reason.

New premier or old, the war was going badly for Japan.
In the beginning of April, the invasion of Okinawa by
Allied troops signified they were no longer knocking at the
outer door, but were opening the inner door. A month
later, the German armies surrendered, leaving Japan alone
in the war. Less than three months after the amphibious
attack began on Okinawa, the island fell.

The issue of Okinawa had a profound effect on the conduct of the war. Okinawa, the southernmost of the Ryukyus,
had belonged to Japan since 1879 and was no farther from
Kyushu, the farthest south of the four main islands that
make up the Japanese homeland, than Hiroshima is from
Tokyo—just a few hundred miles as the plane flies.

The eighty-three-day fight for Okinawa, the last big land battle of the Pacific war, was another of the "decisive" battles the Japanese military had been promising the people which, when lost, was called meaningless. For the Allies, it was another step forward as they island-hopped ever closer, gaining position for the eventual landings on the Japanese home islands. For the Japanese, it was a do-or-die fight, the last chance to stop or delay the invasion before having to do it on the plains of Tokyo.

The defeat was almost impossible to hide from the people of Japan. How does one say, "We have just lost a large, heavily fortified, and garrisoned island a few hundred miles from home, along with one hundred and ten thousand troops and most of our remaining fighting aircraft and ships," and still make it sound like a victory?

The capture of Okinawa gave the Allies a large piece of real estate close to the Japanese homeland, along with an airfield that could be expanded into a major base.

The capture of Okinawa also had a part in the later decision to use the atomic bomb. A segment of the scientists and others who had a share in the development of the weapon had begun to have second thoughts about the effects of its use. There were small, organized groups of scientists questioning its eventual use against people. The groups had to be small since only a few people knew that the bomb existed, much less what its potential was.

Besides, the B-29, the Air Force's long-range Superfortress successor to the B-17 Flying Fortress, had been put into service in the Pacific—the area for which it was built. On the night of March 9, 325 Marianas-based B-29s flew the three-thousand-mile round trip to Tokyo loaded with almost two-thousand tons of fire bombs and set fire to the capital. The planes flew low so that they would use less fuel and could carry a greater bomb load. By the time they had finished, sixteen square miles of Tokyo and possibly one hundred thousand of its inhabitants had been destroyed. That one night bombing of Tokyo ranked with the bombing of Dresden as the worst air attack ever, at least until Hiroshima.

By the first of May, while the battle for Okinawa was still being fought, the B-29s had made three more raids on Tokyo, damaging over half the city. Because other big industrial cities had also been hit regularly, a feeling was developing that Japan might be knocked out of the war by air and sea power alone, without the expected costly invasion, and for those who knew about it, without the use of the atomic bomb.

For the top strategists in the United States, the furious battle for Okinawa gave a different picture. The Japanese who had fought in the Philippines, in New Guinea, Bougainville, and elsewhere in the islands had put up a tremendous battle, but they had proven even more tenacious and stubborn on Okinawa. Despite overwhelming Allied air and naval superiority, it had taken over a quarter of a million Allied troops eighty-three days to destroy the Japanese garrison. In that time, 110,000 Japanese troops had been killed and 7,400 taken prisoner, while the Allies had lost 49,000, 12,250 killed and missing, 36,000 wounded. During the battle for Okinawa, 7,800 Japanese planes were destroyed along with sixteen ships, including the *Yamato*, the world's largest battleship.

If, thought the Allied brass, the Japanese can defend an island with no lengthy Japanese history and three hundred and fifty miles from the nearest homeland with such fierceness, how much more stubbornly will they defend their own home cities, farms, and villages? Estimates of Allied losses for the projected landings on Kyushu in the fall and on Honshu, near Tokyo, in the spring ranged up to one million men.

Suzuki formed his cabinet, using as many able men as he could get. It was not young—Japan's Oriental heritage includes veneration for the aged; also the younger men were in the armed forces. It was composed of some men who wanted peace, some hard-line militarists, and some men of moderate views.

The cabinet was made up of Suzuki and eighteen other men, some of whom are important to this story, most of whom are not, no matter how weighty their names or positions at the time. The cabinet, in Japan, was not terribly important after years of military rule, and during a war its importance diminished even more. Along with the premier, the men we will refer to often include Korechika Anami, the Minister of War; Hisatsune Sakomizu, the Chief Cabinet Secretary and son-in-law of Welfare Minister Tadahiki Okada; Hiroshi Shimomura, the Director of the Information Bureau; and two others we have mentioned before, Shigenori Togo, Foreign Minister, and Mitsumasa Yonai, Navy Minister.

The difficulty of being politically effective if one's views were not intensely jingoistic cannot be overemphasized. Anyone who did not speak in the terms of the extremists ran the risk of being accused of treason. Hundreds of people were arrested, by orders of Anami, on suspicion of holding end-the-war thoughts. The cabinet was supposed to decide on all matters that came before it unanimously and present its conclusion to the Emperor so that he would not have to bother this revered and august mind about its rights and wrongs.

During this time of intense strain, the military was pushing a new "decisive" battle idea. They would keep the invaders from landing on the homeland's sacred soil, or if that couldn't be done, they would make it so expensive for the Allies that a negotiated peace could be worked out.

At the end of 1943, the Allies met and issued the Cairo Declaration. As Russia was not at war with Japan, she did not sign the declaration, a three-nation agreement signed by Roosevelt, Churchill, and Chiang Kai-shek. This set down a determination to finish the war in the Pacific, to bring unrelenting pressure against Japan, to take back all the territories she had seized or occupied. Manchuria, Formosa, and the Pescadores were to be returned to China, and Korea was to become free and independent. "With these objects in view the three Allies ... will continue to persevere in the serious and prolonged operations necessary to procure the unconditional surrender of Japan."

The words *unconditional surrender* caused trouble then and remained a problem. How conditional was unconditional? How could peace terms be negotiated if one side said terms were unconditional? And where did this leave the Emperor?

About this time, the Emperor was wondering where any policy would leave his empire. The military had protected him, too, from the truth. Only, unlike most other civilians, he had access to a certain amount of information, even if it was the type that was apt to be troubling. The information told him that the Japanese war effort had come to a dead halt. The military said that it was preparing itself for the final battle when it would throw the invaders back into the sea. His information said that the defenders were so badly equipped that all they had were numbers and patriotism. The Navy had few useful ships afloat, and not enough oil to supply these with fuel. The Air Force had stopped training flyers; it didn't have enough aviation fuel to spend it on new recruits. In addition to all the shortages of matériel, guns big and little, ammunition, steel, and concrete, there was a growing and alarming shortage of that most important product: food.

How then could the military talk about its day of destiny or even think in terms of victory? Realistically it couldn't. But realistically it shouldn't have been able to get away with a Pearl Harbor, much less try one.

While Allied bombs, naval shells, and land-based artillery were crumbling the fortifications at Okinawa and Allied ground troops were making painful, hard-fought, foot-by-foot advances, the war in Europe ground to a halt. The Japanese military suddenly remembered that their country had a Foreign Office—something they often forgot—and wondered whether this wouldn't be the time to make a deal with Russia. Maybe they could trade some cruisers or land concessions for Soviet oil; maybe they could buy a guarantee of Soviet nonintervention for other concessions; maybe they could even buy Soviet military help, bringing them in as an ally, making a different kind of axis?

Foreign Minister Togo knew better; he knew he couldn't negotiate from a position of such appalling weakness. And he figured, though he didn't know it officially, that America and Britain must have already worked out a deal with Russia. As a matter of fact, the Yalta agreement of February, 1945, had done just that. The Soviet Union had promised to enter hostilities two to three months after the end of the war in Europe, in return for regaining some of its former territories. Nevertheless, at the Emperor's behest, Togo tried to open negotiations with the Russians.

The situation facing the Japanese government at this time and later is best described by the title of one of a series of books published by the United States Government Printing Office; these books are generally referred to by their initials, *USSBS,* which stand for United States Strategic Bombing Survey. The titles of the individual volumes tell their own story, titles such as *Effects of Strategic Bombing on Japanese Morale* and *The Effects of Atomic Bombs on Hiroshima and Nagasaki.* One volume's title is *Japan's Struggle to End the War.* The key word here is *struggle.*

As conditions continued to become worse for the Japanese, another group came to the fore. Known as the Supreme Council for the Direction of the War, it consisted of the Premier, Foreign Minister, Ministers of War and Navy, and Chiefs of the General Staffs of the Army and the Navy (these latter two not being members of the cabinet). In existence since mid-1944, it, like many groups, was run, in general, by a group of military and civilian aides and accomplished very little. In May, the group changed its composition to a certain extent, first by deciding to meet alone, the principals only, without their secretaries and aides, since their previous meeting had developed into almost rubber-stamped approvals of decisions arrived at by these same aides. Also a new Navy Chief of Staff became a member of the Big Six.

These six men were most important; they formed the "inner cabinet" which made decisions at the highest level for the cabinet, and then for the Emperor, to approve. They were Premier Suzuki, of course; Foreign Minister Togo; War Minister Korechika Anami, who was the most powerful man in Japan at the time; Navy Minister Yonai; Army Chief of Staff Yoshijiro Umezu, who looked like an Oriental Mussolini and was more dictatorial; and Navy Chief of Staff Soemu Toyoda, an eloquent, sixty-year-old xenophobe. He was put in by Suzuki to replace Oikawa, the earlier member, because Toyoda belonged to the same general clan as Anami and Umezu, and the Premier thought he would be able to help turn the two Army men from their hard-line attitude.

Although the possibility of offering other peace feelers was not completely ignored, the Japanese turned their real hopes toward Moscow. Historically, asking the Soviet Union to intercede in the behalf of Japan seemed about as likely of success as asking a Montague to speak for a Capulet or a Hatfield for a McCoy.

The three major Asian powers were China, Russia, and Japan. Russia and Japan got in each other's way consistently once Japan had turned away from her isolationist stance.

But Japan's early audacious military successes on the mainland had given her a large amount of land that could be used for bargaining. In addition, anything looked better at the time than the prospect of unconditional surrender.

Various individuals approached American and British representatives in the neutral countries, particularly in Switzerland and Sweden. These individuals were usually Japanese diplomatic or military representatives who, having spent some time in the West, wanted to save their country from certain destruction. The trouble was that they were not authorized to do anything, and peace efforts always broke down when authority to speak or negotiate for the government in Tokyo was denied.

However, after V-E Day, with no Japanese leverage possible by serving as a mediator between Russia and Germany, Koki Hirota, a former premier and former ambassador to Moscow, was asked to speak to Jacob Malik, Soviet ambassador to Tokyo. He did so, prepared to offer a few options: any kind of agreement to keep Russia from eventually entering the war against Japan; a new nonaggression treaty, with the possibility of Soviet aid; as a last resort, a request for the Soviet Union to act as an honest broker between Japan and the Allies to end the war in the Pacific.

Hirota did this early in June, in a studiously impromptu fashion, so that if nothing came of them, these could be considered informal talks. Malik did not appear to be impressed; he wanted to be reassured that this was the feeling of the government and of the people, both of whom had a long record of hostility. The whole Japanese ploy with Russia, which was pursued up to August 8, ran into the same brick wall of resistance because Russia was already committed to a different kind of action.

The Japanese military were split on how to end the war. One group was the fight-to-the-end faction, better death than the dishonor of losing; the other faction was advocating an all-out defense of the home islands so that better terms could be negotiated. No one was heard to say that the wise thing to do would be to stop now before the whole island and most of its people were destroyed. And these discussions were being held after the March fire-bombing of Tokyo, during the period when the B-29s were bombing the main cities without encountering any significant fighter opposition. Some of the Japanese leaders knew that their country had no military chance at all, but most of the others, believers in their own propaganda or unwilling to face facts, spoke or acted as though there was still a possibility of victory if the people would stand together.

By June, a policy statement had been issued, exhorting the whole nation to fight to the end as one man. This satisfied the military, did no good at all, and gave the Allied brass the impression that all the civilians were now, in effect, a part of the military and fair targets. Allied bombing, pre-Hiroshima, hit civilian concentrations as well as strategic military targets. The theory behind this was that in addition to having heavy industry complexes, the Japanese war and industrial machine was split into small subcontracting units, many of which were, in effect, "cottage industries" which had to be rooted out if the capacity to make war was to be destroyed or reduced. Or, so went the story.

And during this time, the 509th Composite Group was moving from Wendover Field, Utah, to its segregated quarters on Tinian, and selected B-29s from its small bomb group were making training flights over Japan, flying singly or with another B-29, or two, as observation escort, and from extreme altitudes for those days, thirty thousand feet or more, dropping huge, oddly shaped single bombs, filled with conventional explosives. If the Japanese had known the purpose of these flights, would their plans have changed? Probably not, as they wouldn't have believed what they learned.

CHAPTER III

Mokusatsu Snafu

The Japanese were not the only ones who wouldn't have believed it; neither, at that time, would many Americans, had
they heard of the atomic bomb, which they hadn't. And
even military and political figures who were in a position
to know about it remained unconvinced of its practicability
or its success. Among these was the President's military adviser, Admiral Leahy.

While the battle for Okinawa was just getting into high
gear, President Roosevelt died suddenly at Warm Springs,
Georgia. He was succeeded at once by Harry S Truman
who, as Vice-President, knew nothing officially of the Manhattan Project and the new weapon. At the close of a meeting soon after he was sworn in as the new President,
Truman was told by Secretary of War Stimson that he had
to see him about something. After the others had left,
Stimson told the new President about the bomb.

Earlier, when he had been a senator heading an important
investigative committee, Truman had come upon rumors
of such a huge new development and had started to have it
looked into. At that time, Secretary Stimson visited him to

ask him to call off his dogs. Upon being assured that the new project was legitimate Truman told the secretary that because of his high regard for the older man, there would be no more investigation.

Plans were being made in the Allied capitals in June, 1945, for the upcoming Potsdam Conference, to discuss problems resulting from the end of the Euorpean war and to settle final plans to end the one in the Pacific. Despite Hirota's earlier lack of success with Ambassador Malik, he tried again, also without results. Marquis Kido then urged the Emperor to think about making an effort to end the war by using the Soviet Union as an intermediary. Suzuki and Kido convinced the Emperor to ask Prince Konoye to go to Moscow, with carte blanche to negotiate. But as all this took time, it was obvious that Foreign Minister Molotov and Premier Stalin would be en route to Potsdam by the time Konoye arrived.

It is difficult to understand, with hindsight, the continued reliance on the possibility of help from the Russian government. The only explanation is the example of the drowning man clutching at straws. The island empire was drowning in a sea of troubles, most of them brought about by their own actions or customs. A direct approach to Britain or the United States would probably have been more effective, but they were afraid to risk it. The military hard-liners would have considered it treason and would have had a certain amount of popular backing in their view, as the term *unconditional surrender,* insisted on by the Allies, didn't seem to leave much room for negotiation.

Despite the fact that there was no past history of success to give hope that a plea to the Soviet Union would be useful, Prince Konoye was asked by the Emperor to go to Moscow as soon as possible, acting as a special envoy from the Throne. With the Potsdam meeting under way, Japanese Ambassador Sato was requested to make arrangements for

Prince Konoye and his staff to visit Moscow and see the Soviet leaders as soon as they returned from Potsdam.

The diplomats were meeting at Potsdam when the world's first atomic bomb was tried out in the Trinity test at Alamogordo. After President Truman had been given coded word that the successful test exceeded all expectations, he worried about whether to tell Premier Stalin about it. Because of the Soviet's spies at Los Alamos and Alamogordo, the chances are that Truman's worries were, like many worries, completely unnecessary. Stalin probably knew the results almost as soon as Truman did. At any rate, at one meeting, before the conference broke up, Truman wandered over to Stalin and told him informally that a new and very powerful weapon had been developed. Stalin said he hoped it would be used against the Japanese, and there the matter rested. Truman felt he had done his part; when the bomb was used, the Russians couldn't say they hadn't been told about it.

The Potsdam Conference ended, and a proclamation was issued, about and to Japan. The Cairo Declaration of September, 1943, already had laid down certain conditions, mainly that Japan would be stripped of all Pacific islands she had seized or occupied since 1914, would restore territories stolen from China, and would be expelled from other territories taken by violence.

It also stated that the Allies would persevere in the operations necessary to procure the unconditional surrender of Japan. The Yalta agreement of February, 1945, spelled out further details, including the promise of Russia's involvement in the war against Japan within three months of the surrender of Germany and Russian aid to help China get rid of the Japanese invaders, in return for which Russia would get back various territories and rights in the area lost since 1904.

The Potsdam statement of July 26, 1945, gave more details. Since Russia at that time was officially at peace with

Japan, this was a joint statement of just the United States, China, and Great Britain. The Yalta agreement had been signed by Stalin, Roosevelt, and Churchill five and a half months earlier, but had not yet been released to the world. The Potsdam statement, not as factual, was mainly a propaganda paper, giving the Japanese reasons to surrender. It said that the three heads of state, representing the millions of their countrymen, agreed that Japan should be given an opportunity to end the war. Japan was told that the combined land, sea, and air forces of the three nations, reinforced from the west, were poised to strike the final blows. What happened to Germany as a result of her "futile and senseless resistance" was given as an example of what would happen to Japan, meaning the complete destruction of Japanese armed forces and the utter devastation of the Japanese homeland. It said that Japan had to decide whether she would be controlled by the militarists who had brought Japan to the brink of annihilation or to follow the course of reason.

The statement included these terms: The influence of those who have misled Japan into a course of world conquest must be eliminated for all time; until a new order of peace, security, and justice is secured, the Allies will occupy points in Japan; Japan's sovereignty will be limited to the four main islands (Honshu, Hokkaido, Kyushu, Shikoku) and some minor islands to be determined; the Japanese military forces after being disarmed shall be allowed to return home; stern justice shall be meted out to war criminals; freedom of speech, religion, thought, and respect for human rights shall be established; Japanese industries shall remain but not those allowing her to rearm; the occupying forces shall be withdrawn as soon as these objectives have been accomplished and a peaceful and responsible government has been established in accordance with the freely expressed will of the

Japanese people. The statement ends with a brief paragraph:

"We call upon the government of Japan to proclaim now the unconditional surrender of all Japanese armed forces, and to provide proper and adequate assurances of their good faith and action. The alternative for Japan is prompt and utter destruction."

The Yalta agreement offered Russia inducements to enter the war against Japan; the Potsdam meeting was held in an attempt to settle several matters about Europe and to make sure that Russia would fulfill its commitment in the Pacific. From the standpoint of hindsight, it is evident that much more pressure would have had to be brought to prevent Russia from entering the Pacific war than was ever exerted to bring her in. Similarly, President Truman has been criticized for being so generous to the Russians at Potsdam when it was evident we were well on the way to beating Japan without Russian help.

In President Truman's defense, it must be mentioned that he was under pressure from the military to get all the Russian help he could. For one thing, practically no one knew about the atomic bomb at the time, and those who did, particularly the military men who did, had no faith in its efficacy. Since the planned invasion of Japan was expected to take a heavy toll of the attackers, American and British brass wanted the pressure relieved by a Russian attack in Manchuria and the threat of invasion from the north and west.

There is a significant but innocent-appearing change in the wording of the Potsdam statement as compared with earlier ones. While the previous declarations had spoken about the unconditional surrender of Japan, the Potsdam statement spoke of the unconditional surrender of Japanese armed forces. In the rarefied world of diplomatic language, this was a change that was made with a good deal of thought and discussion. There were those in the United States who wanted reference to unconditional surrender dropped completely, but it could not be done. It was feared that any American politician who softened the terms to Japan would never be able to live it down. To compensate for this, President Truman tried to spell out what he meant by *unconditional surrender* in his end-of-the-war-in-Europe statement in May, in which he emphasized that this was a military surrender and did not include the extermination or enslavement of the Japanese people.

Of course, what all these statements left out was the crucial issue: What was to be the position of the Emperor?

If it was politically improbable for an American politician to soften the terms of unconditional surrender, it would have been impossible, the recent past having been what it had been, to give the Japanese any assurance that its royal house would remain in power. Actually, Secretary of War Stimson had tried to do just that when he drafted a memorandum for the President designed to provide a means to victory without invasion. In it, he included the statement that the Allies would not preclude the present dynasty from serving as a constitutional monarchy. Most of the Stimson memorandum was incorporated into the Potsdam statement, but this part was dropped, partly at the insistence of Secretary of State Byrnes and former Secretary Hull.

This is just one of a series of "might-have-beens" that took place about this time. President Truman obviously felt that the Potsdam proclamation was a just and fair-minded document that gave the Japanese government an opportunity to get out of a hopeless situation without further damage to the nation, beyond that of admitting that it had lost a war it never should have started. He expected a reaction from Tokyo, a favorable one; what else could they do?

The Japanese government heard officially of the Potsdam

proclamation the day after it had been signed and released. The Tokyo overseas radio bureau picked it up from a San Francisco broadcast. The Foreign Office immediately started studying the rough draft of the broadcast while an official translation was being worked up. The proclamation set up immediate problems for the Foreign Office: how to answer it, how to get around anticipated Army opposition, how to tell the Japanese people about it.

Shunichi Matsumoto, the second man in the Foreign Ministry, wanted to accept the terms as stated. He set to work drafting a reply to be sent to the Japanese ministers in neutral capitals, for transmittal to the Allies. But Foreign Minister Togo was more cautious, though he, too, believed that Japan would have to accept the terms offered. Togo felt that the word change from plain *unconditional surrender* to *unconditional surrender of the armed forces* indicated that a further compromise, more acceptable to the military, might be possible and that another appeal to the Soviet Union's good offices might be worthwhile.

Accordingly, the Supreme War Council was called in to a 10:30 A.M. meeting, July 27, to consider an answer. As this was a diplomatic question at the moment, Shigenori Togo took the lead. He pointed out the change in wording and talked the other five members of the Big Six into withholding an official reply until Moscow was heard from.

That afternoon a full cabinet meeting was held to try to work out a way to tell the Japanese people the contents of the Potsdam statement. Togo said that no announcement should be made until the government had decided how it was going to treat it. There were objections to this delaying action, based on the fact that since the rest of the world knew about the proclamation, sooner or later the Japanese people would know about it, too. In addition, delay might appear to the rest of the world to be an example of Japanese weakness. The Army, through Gen. Korechika Anami, the

War Minister, gave its conditions. If news of the proclamation were to be released, the government at the same time must announce its attitude toward the terms, indicating the attitude it wanted the people to take. That, of course, was the point of view of people accustomed to managing the news.

The meeting ended, as might have been forecast, with a compromise. The news would be released, but it would be played down; the proclamation itself would not be published, only paraphrased without any editorial comment. Among the items left out were the sentences about the armed forces being allowed to return home after being disarmed and the crucial "We do not intend that the Japanese shall be enslaved as a race or destroyed as a nation."

In other words, while stalling for time, despite the proclamation's "we shall brook no delay" warning, the Japanese government would soft pedal the news. What came after that could be regarded as an almost classic example of how to mess up delicate matters in the worst possible way. In addition to making an error of judgment—the Japanese thought they had time to shilly-shally, to look for a way out—they committed a semantic error that may have led to the use of the atomic bombs against their cities. It did not cause the bombs to be used, but it was a contributing factor, and a different word use and action might have made for a different American decision. Because by that time, it would have taken a strong negative action by President Truman to have stopped the use of the bomb.

The decision of the cabinet was to delay a reaction to the proclamation. This seemed to suit Premier Suzuki well; at this stage in life, he was not a man to make a strong decision, to take a strong stand. He had been content to let the younger (sixty-two) foreign minister, Togo, carry the ball at the Big Six and full cabinet meetings. Suzuki said the government would *mokusatsu* the proclamation.

This word, which comes from the combination of two roots—*moku*, meaning "silent," and *satsu*, meaning "kill"— has two meanings, quite similar but with shades of difference that would cause trouble. Literally, it means "to kill with silence." A dictionary definition is "to take no notice of, ignore, treat with silent contempt." But it also means "to remain in a wise and masterly inactivity." The conjecture is that the latter meaning is what Suzuki had in mind, but the error was compounded.

The Japanese papers the next day (Saturday, July 28) picked up the word in their front-page stories, using it in the context of treating with silent contempt. A lead story in Tokyo's *Asahi Shimbun* said that as the joint declaration was of no great value, it would serve only to re-enhance the government's resolve to carry the war forward unfalteringly to a successful conclusion.

At a meeting that morning, the Army and Navy Chiefs of Staff and the War Minister demanded a positive refutation or denunciation of the Potsdam proclamation. This was an indication of what was to become an open split, with Anami, Umezu, and Toyoda, the bitter-end hawks, pitted against Yonai, Togo, and (sometimes) Suzuki. The hawks said that an immediate statement of rejection of the terms would have to be issued in order to bolster the morale of the troops. Admiral Yonai tried to curb his colleagues' impatience, but wasn't too successful. Neither Togo nor Suzuki was present at that meeting; whether this had any effect on the Premier is hard to say. But when he held a press conference that afternoon, he said that he considered the Potsdam statement a repeat of the Cairo Declaration, that the government viewed it as a "thing of no great value, we will simply *mokusatsu* it. We will press forward resolutely to carry the war to a successful conclusion."

This had not been the sense of the meetings of the full cabinet or the previous "inner cabinet," and Foreign Minister Togo was reputedly fit to be tied when he read Suzuki's remarks, but there was nothing he could do about them at that time. The original idea of saying nothing about the terms of the Potsdam proclamation would not have been effective. Not only was the radio repeating the story by short-wave, but powerful Allied transmitters on Saipan and other islands were beaming the story to the Japanese people on conventional medium waves. With effectual control of the air, Allied planes were dropping leaflets by the thousands, with the full terms of the invitation for the Japanese to end the war spelled out in Japanese. Of course, it was forbidden for the Japanese to pick up, read, or pass on these leaflets or the information on them. The Japanese people were extremely obedient and well trained. They were also curious, and despite the best government efforts, fearful. Enough of these leaflets were read and talked about for the news to be spread.

In many other countries there might have been revolts or threats to the government from a people who had sacrificed and uncomplainingly borne a heavy burden. In Japan, the threat to the government came from the military. It was the military who had to be appeased, not the people. The government could not say to the Allies: We don't like the terms, but we accept them because there's nothing else we can do. Instead, more urgent messages were sent to Ambassador Sato in Moscow, who went through the hopeless motions of trying to pressure the Kremlin to use its good offices. Sato got nowhere and reported to Togo that the only thing Japan could do was accept the Potsdam terms and hope for the best. Togo knew that he would not be able to persuade the military either to accept the terms or to deal directly with the Americans and British.

Minister of War Anami was not blind enough to think that the Japanese could win at this late date. But he did want to see the war continued at least until the Allies landed on Kyushu. He had several reasons for this; it is impossible to say which ones predominated. They included the Samurai's view that one doesn't surrender; if one has to go down, he goes down fighting. An Allied landing on Kyushu might be inevitable, but it could be made so costly for the invaders that better terms than unconditional surrender might be arranged. Anami also was playing on American fears of the Soviet Union. He figured that the moment American troops landed on Japan, Russian troops would also attack and the Americans would be eager to conclude a peace treaty rather than see the Russians occupy much of the Asian mainland and part of the Japanese islands.

The Japanese cabinet had met and had decided the thing to do was to postpone an immediate answer while trying to figure out a way to present defeat to the people, but Suzuki's remarks had changed all that. There has been speculation that the military establishment was responsible for Suzuki's statement and the way it was played up in the press, but there is no evidence to support this, and a good deal against it. Nevertheless the news had gone out, and the feeling in the world at large, and in Washington in particular, was that the Japanese government had rejected the terms completely. Not only had rejected them, but had done so in a manner that signified they were beneath consideration.

Actually, for several days Japan officially did nothing. Or nothing constructive. Her people suffered. The air raids continued unabated, food was harder to come by, medical supplies became scarcer, and the brass publicly talked big about the shore defenses and costs to the enemy if an invasion should be tried and privately wondered how it could get the materials necessary to build primitive antilanding devices. The Allies, having put their invasion plans on paper, were moving troops and equipment, going through all the complicated logistical motions preparatory to large-scale amphibious war.

On the little Mariana island of Tinian, the cruiser *Indianapolis* had delivered a small shipment of atomic material with a large amount of destructive power, and had promptly been sunk in the Philippine Sea by a Japanese submarine. The *Indianapolis,* after a record-breaking run from the West Coast of America, had unloaded its precious cargo quite simply at Tinian. While guards ostentatiously protected some large crates being taken from the cruiser, two men casually left the ship's stern carrying a couple of very heavy but innocent-looking buckets, got into a launch, and turned over their precious cargo to a group of waiting technicians.

In Washington, Secretary of War Stimson, waiting anxiously for a reaction to the Potsdam conditions, received only newspaper reports saying the government of Japan had not even bothered to reject the proclamation. Later, he wrote that the United States could only demonstrate that the ultimatum had meant what it said, that continuation of the war would bring about the destruction of the Japanese armed forces and utter devastation of the Japanese homeland. For such a purpose the atomic bomb was an eminently suitable weapon.

The proclamation had been signed and released to the world on July 26, the day after Clement Attlee replaced Winston Churchill as Britain's prime minister and representative at Potsdam. Premier Suzuki's press conference, at which he compounded his *mokusatsu* error, was held on July 28, a Saturday. Full reports of it appeared in Japanese papers on Monday, July 30, and elsewhere in the world. Ambassador Sato, still pushing his hopeless task in Moscow, tried again to get an answer from the Kremlin, this time being able to refer to the Potsdam proclamation, saying that of course unconditional surrender was out of the question, but that his government was open to various forms of compromise to end the war.

This is an example of diplomatic double-talk, because

while he was telling this to the Soviet Vice Foreign Commissar, he was cabling back to Minister Togo that the only way Japan could get out of the war was by unconditional surrender, to which Togo answered sharply that Japan didn't need Russian help to do that. All the cables, the entire Japanese effort to get Soviet aid, were known to United States officials, both from Russian sources and, generally before that, from the cables themselves.

For some time the United States had been obtaining useful and useless material from Japanese communications, having earlier cracked the code the Japanese were using. Benefiting from a combination of blunders on both sides, America continued to get this information even after the codes were changed. The first blunder was American. Some OSS agents reportedly broke into the Japanese embassy at Lisbon so carelessly that the Japanese discovered it and decided, of course, to change the code. Then they did something so classically stupid, it is almost unbelievable. Using the old code they thought might have been stolen, they sent word that a new code would be substituted. By listening and translating, our cryptographers learned when and how at least one new code book was being shipped. The American Navy went after the ship and sank it, a diver went down and brought up the new code book, and hardly a message was lost. What Ambassador Sato thought he was saying in private to Minister Togo was soon known in Washington.

For nearly a week, while waiting for a definite answer from Moscow, the Japanese government seemed to be in a state of suspended animation. While officials scurried about, attending their never-ending series of meetings, nothing was done; there was no official reply to the Potsdam proclamation. The *mokusatsu* idea, treat it with silence while trying to formulate a policy, became a policy in itself. Meanwhile, the lines were growing firmer. Not the lines of defense. Despite what was being said, there wasn't enough metal and

concrete available to make the defenses firm enough to with-
stand a determined, well-supplied invasion. What got firmer
were the positions of the no-surrender, fight-to-the-death
group and the opposing peace-at-any-price group.

This, of course, was behind the scenes. Japan had no tradition of open debate on national issues, besides having been
accustomed for too long to being told what to do by the
military. The people were suffering; they had been through
much and conditions were getting worse. But most of them
were not accustomed to much; they had lived in an agri-
cultural nation, only lately turned to industry, and were
inured to the vicissitudes of nature and man. They were intensely patriotic and loyal, both to their nation and to the
Emperor. They went, from day to day, through the motions
of their work, hoping for a word from absent sons or husbands in the armed forces, scraping by on little food, wish-
ing for a good night's sleep, cutting lanes through the towns
and cities to act as firebreaks, taking care of their young and
old, and mostly waiting. Waiting for what? They didn't
know, for some kind of divine intervention that would ease
their condition.

The government was acting the way a bird is supposed to
when frightened and fascinated into inaction by a snake.
The activists, led by Anami, were satisfied. They were
getting just what they wanted—no answer to the proclamation, which was equivalent to a no.

But while the Japanese were postponing action, they got
an answer to their no answer—the atomic bomb at Hiroshima.

First reports of the catastrophe at Hiroshima, which took
place at 0815 local time, as people were starting to work,
reached Tokyo at about noon. It was a Domei News Bureau
report without any details. By evening more details came
in, saying that Hiroshima had been badly damaged by a
small number of planes using a new type of bomb. The next

morning, there was a single descriptive sentence: "The whole city of Hiroshima was destroyed instantly by a single bomb."

This fairly accurate statement had one immediate effect: The Supreme Command clamped on tight censorship and flew in an investigative team. What they saw in Hiroshima, the crew of the *Enola Gay* could have told them a few minutes after the bomb had been dropped and detonated. As of then, Hiroshima no longer existed as a living, functioning city.

President Truman, on getting news of the successful mission while en route home from Potsdam, had a previously prepared statement released to the press. It was beamed to Japan by radio and, like the Potsdam proclamation, also put into print, in the form of a Japanese tabloid newspaper, and dropped all over the island empire as soon as possible.

In Japan, the military, trying to put the best possible face on an unmistakable disaster, made an attempt to convince itself that there could be only one of these new bombs, that it must have been a lucky hit of some kind—and that whatever it was, the people shouldn't be allowed to know about it.

But the officials knew about it. Foreign Minister Togo told the entire cabinet what had happened at Hiroshima; they listened and did nothing. Then Togo took it up with the Emperor, who said that Japan must accept the inevitable. The inability to move and make obvious decisions which had held the government in thrall for several days continued despite this new and dramatic threat to the country's existence. Premier Suzuki called for an emergency meeting of the Supreme War Council, a meeting that had to be postponed because one of the Big Six had some pressing business and could not attend!

If the men on the *Enola Gay* had heard about that, they would have been amazed. Having seen what they had of the death of the city, they half expected to hear of the end of the war while they were on their way back to Tinian. No government, they felt, could subject its land and people to such destruction. They didn't realize that most of the Japanese people didn't know what had happened at Hiroshima, that many Japanese didn't even know what had happened to Tokyo almost five months before.

They also didn't realize another phenomenon of the atomic bomb—unless one were there to see it for himself, he would be unable to believe the destruction it causes. After the men of the 509th had returned to Tinian after being debriefed, Truman released word to the world. For the first time, these men were free to talk a little about what they had been doing. People listened and agreed, but few could visualize the destructive power of the new weapon, could comprehend its magnitude.

To most people, having to take in the idea as a practicality rather than wild, off-in-the-future theory, it just seemed to be a larger, more powerful bomb than the old ones. Even the measuring of its force, "a single bomb with the destructive power of 20,000 tons of TNT," made it seem like a much more powerful but still conventional weapon. Not only did it have the destructive, explosive power of tons of TNT, it instantaneously released a heat greater than man had ever before experienced, a pressure that drove buildings straight down into the ground, and radiation that affected every living thing within wide areas.

But how could soldiers fighting a war realize this? How could statesmen and politicians, in Washington, Moscow, or Tokyo realize this? A few of them, in Washington, had been told of the destructive capabilities of the new bomb, and there were secret pictures available of the test shot at Alamogordo, but these were static photos of destruction on the desert that could give no real indication to the untrained of the total havoc created. Even the brilliant J. Robert Oppenheimer, the man in charge of the scientific development of the bomb, underestimated the casualty total by approximately 80 percent.

It is doubtful whether there were a hundred men on this planet, outside of those who had lived through the first twenty-four hours after the Hiroshima detonation, who truly understood the implications of that first atomic blast, and most of the Hiroshima survivors were either too numbed or untrained to understand. Besides, the truth was so horrifying that they could not take it in. Almost every survivor thought it must have been detonated very close to him and that what happened after was the result of fire.

Following the release of the bomb from the *Enola Gay's* bomb bay, some instrument packages were parachuted down from the accompanying instrument plane. A few people saw these small parachutes descending and later thought they contained something responsible for the terrible damage. They didn't; they were only supposed to record the damage. But the general confusion about the bomb, despite the description released in Washington, gave the Japanese bitter-enders an opportunity to continue their procrastination.

Not the Emperor, though. When Foreign Minister Togo gave him a fairly complete report of what had happened at Hiroshima, he told Togo to inform Premier Suzuki that with this new type of weapon being used against Japan, she was powerless to continue the war and must try to stop it at once. Hiroshima should not be repeated.

That was August 8. At that time, on Guam, a Top Secret Field Order was issued calling for another Special Bombing Mission. Whereas the first one had named three possible targets, with Hiroshima the primary one, this only listed two. Primary was the Kokura arsenal; the secondary target was the Mitsubishi works and the Nagasaki urban area.

About this time, in Osaka, a young American flyer, Lt. Marcus McDilda, was being interrogated. His Iwo Jima–

based P-51 had been shot down while on a strafing mission. He had escaped, bruised and shaken but alive. His interrogation was more or less routine until he was asked what he knew about the atomic bomb used on Hiroshima. As he knew nothing about it except talk he'd picked up on Iwo after its use, he said so. They pressed their questioning, reportedly punctuating their questions with blows. When an officer came in with a sword and threatened to cut off his head if he didn't tell them about the bomb, he made up an ingenious story that wouldn't have fooled a chemist or physicist or today's nuclear-conscious children, but at the time would have passed as a possibility in most of America, as well as in Japan.

His description of how the bomb worked, as well as its size, was pure fabrication, as was his answer when asked where it would be used next. He knew even less about that than how the bomb worked, but since he could figure out what they wouldn't like to hear, he said he understood it was to be Kyoto or Tokyo, Tokyo within the next few days. Kyoto, as we know, had been put on the original target list and taken off repeatedly, finally for good, by Secretary Stimson. Tokyo actually would have been the primary target for the third bomb.

The American prisoner's information was telephoned to the secret police in Tokyo.

CHAPTER IV

The Other Shoe

The day before, in Moscow, Ambassador Sato had received some of the news for which he had been waiting—Foreign Commissar Molotov let him know that he could have an audience at 11 P.M. the following evening, a time which was later advanced by three hours. Ambassador Sato began with the usual diplomatic formalities, congratulating the commissar on his trip to Potsdam and safe return, but was interrupted quickly by Molotov who may not have wanted to be embarrassed by too many niceties, considering the news he was about to give the ambassador.

Molotov said he had a notification for the Japanese government, which he began to read aloud. It said, in effect, that since Japan was now the only great power still standing for the continuation of the war and that since Japan had rejected the Potsdam demand for surrender, her request to the Soviet Union to act as a mediator had therefore lost its foundation. With Japan's refusal to capitulate, the Allies had approached the Soviet government to join with them in the war against Japanese aggression. True to its obligation as an Ally, the Soviet government had accepted and joined in the July 26 declaration; starting the next day (August 9) the Soviet government would consider herself in a state of war with Japan.

Sato cabled this unwelcome news to Togo. By the time it was received, Russian armies had started (1 A.M. August 9, Tokyo time) across the Manchurian border to annihilate the Kwantung Army. The existence and strength of this group is another example of the misleading or erroneous intelligence work that plagued both sides of this war. For years the impression had been built up throughout the world that this was an extremely powerful, self-contained army. At one time it had probably been true. But during 1944, the Japanese Supreme Command had started moving some of the Kwantung Army's best troops and equipment back to the homeland for possible use in the eventual defense of the islands. In some way, either this was not known to the Allies or its extent was not acknowledged by them because one of the major reasons for putting pressure on Russia to enter the Pacific war at Yalta, and even as late as at Potsdam, was the respect of the American brass for the Kwantung Army. It was described as being the cream of the Japanese Army, an independent force with its own autonomous command and industrial base. Manchuria was big and rich enough in natural resources to provide much that the Army needed. It was felt that this army alone was capable of prolonging the war even after the Japanese islands had been subdued, unless Russia should come in and engage it.

There was a peculiar sort of reverse parallel between the Kwantung Army and the atomic-bombing 509th Composite Group. The Kwantung Army, which had been huge, was important, more because of past publicity than because of present capability. The 509th Composite Group, which was also self-sufficient and semiautonomous, comprised less than two thousand men. It had a tremendous potential. Not only was it unpublicized and unknown to the general public, but its very existence was a secret. This was expected to magnify its effectiveness when it went to work.

At least one group of Japanese knew of the unit's existence on Tinian—the radio monitors outside of Tokyo had reported a new signal from the Marianas, but that didn't mean anything; it could have been any kind of a group. There was also the possibility that there were Japanese stragglers hiding out in the hills of Tinian with a shortwave radio transmitter. All they could have reported, however, was that a new outfit had landed on the island—even the other American units on the island didn't know any more than that, except that whatever the 509th was up to, it wasn't talking about it.

The original plans for use of the atomic bomb had been to drop two of them in rapid succession, the feeling being that one might be considered a freak, but that two should convince anyone that the United States had the capability of delivering a series of punches, any one of which could be a knockout. The problem was a shortage of nuclear material, and though only a few pounds of it was needed in the warhead of a bomb, its availability was measured in milligrams. Enough uranium 235 had been promised for the initial bomb by the first of August, along with enough newly discovered plutonium, to arm the second bomb at about the same time. More plutonium, enough for a third and a fourth bomb, was "in the pipeline" and would be available in a few days or weeks.

The question of whether or not to use the bomb, and when, had been on the minds of many of the men who knew about it, ever since the scientists had decided that the new weapon would probably work. Secretary of War Stimson reported this at some length in several papers and interviews, as well as in his book *On Active Service in War and Peace,* written with McGeorge Bundy. Stimson had served his country well, in many capacities, for a long period. He was what would be considered today a traditionalist, a leading member of the Establishment. He was also a man of intelligence, sensitivity, and conscience. He conducted a lengthy interior dialogue about the use of the bomb and came to the conclusion that it should be used, if necessary.

President Truman, a man given to blunt truth-telling, has said he never lost any sleep over the decision, a statement which is hard to believe. When the Manhattan Project was initiated to build the bomb, no one was worrying too much about whether it should be used; the worry was whether or not it could be made and whether it would work.

At that time, conditions were far different. What became the Manhattan Project was started not because the military wanted it—at the time they were not thinking about the feasibility of atomic power in a bomb—but because a group of civilian scientists, many of them émigrés from dictator-ridden Europe, was afraid that Hitler and the Nazi scientists would capitalize on this powerful weapon and come up with it first, making their military machine an even worse threat to the rest of the world than it already was. This was in 1939. Several of these scientists went to Dr. Albert Einstein and persuaded him to write a letter to President Roosevelt explaining the problem and asking for government help to provide limited funds for research.

What happened after Roosevelt's interest was aroused is a fascinating story that has been told often. What began as a scientist's theory turned into a gigantic and secret undertaking that was, in the opinion of many, a tremendous gamble. As with any new undertaking, there were opposing views as to its practicability. Even Dr. Einstein in his original letter, while stating that an explosive of unprecedented power could be built, said it would have to be so large that it would not be possible to deliver it by plane. It became obvious, as one difficulty after another was encountered and surmounted, that though the project had been started as a race against the German scientists and engineers, the likelihood was that the war in Europe would be over before the bomb would be available for use. Work was continued, however, so that it could be used against the Japanese as soon as possible.

There has been speculation in recent years that America would never have used the bomb in Europe, that with our "white bias" we would not have used this weapon against a European people. This is nonsense, as is much after-the-fact talk. Work on the bomb—not the building of the bomb, but experimental, small-scale research—was started before we were in the war, to beat the Nazis to it. During the Battle of the Bulge in December, 1944, President Roosevelt called in General Groves to ask whether the delivery date for the atomic bomb couldn't be moved up from August 1 so that it could be used against the desperate Nazi counteroffensive. General Groves had to say no; even the August date was a target rather than a certainty.

Besides, General Groves was not sure that the bomb, if built, would work. Although outwardly giving an air of confidence, he later admitted that he figured it had about a 60 percent chance of being effective. General Groves, an Army builder and administrator, was in charge of the project, along with Dr. Oppenheimer, the scientific head. There was a gulf between many of the Army people and technicians and the scientists, who were thought of as "longhairs."

After the European phase of the war ended, some of the scientists working on the bomb project began to have second thoughts about the Pandora's box they were opening. At first it had been a challenge, an attempt to do something that had never before been done and perhaps couldn't be done, an expansion of man's knowledge and imagination. But as success grew more certain, many began to wonder about the morality of using such a weapon. A number of

sincere, patriotic, and dedicated scientists signed the so-
called Franck Report which asked that some alternative be
found to the use of the bomb against people.

There were committees for and against, polls taken,
speeches made, and papers written on the subject—all within
a small circle and in the strictest secrecy. Generally speaking, the military thought this controversy was a lot of nonsense, a tempest in a teapot, the kind of thing that occurs
when civilians, particularly impractical scientists, interfere
in the conduct of martial affairs. Some of the military people
objected for a different reason—they did not think the bomb
would work or, if it worked, would have the effect the
scientists thought it would. And who could tell? This was
something so new and different that there were no standards
of comparison.

Secretary of War Stimson, as we have said, was a thought-
ful and sensitive man, and he was worrying about the use
of the bomb. Although the ultimate decision rested with
President Truman, it was up to Stimson to advise him, and
to advise him correctly. Stimson, who had come to his own
conclusions, had helped set up an interim committee to
look into problems connected with the use of the bomb.
This committee was composed entirely of civilians in order
to avoid possible military bias and had an advisory scientific
panel made up of a few of the project's scientific leaders.

The moral and ethical questions were great. The questions were numerous, including whether any preannouncement of the use of the bomb should be given to the
population to be affected by it. It became difficult to separate
the moral and ethical issues from the purely military, as
exemplified in the question of the preannouncement. Suppose, said the military, we were to say that we are going to
detonate the greatest man-made explosion the world has
ever seen at 8:15 A.M. over Second Army Headquarters at
Hiroshima. What would happen if the mission were aborted

by weather, mechanical failure, or something like that? What if the bomb were to be dropped and didn't detonate as planned? Would we lose the psychological shock value of this new weapon if it worked perfectly but we talked about it beforehand? What, asked Secretary Byrnes, was to prevent the Japanese from shifting Allied prisoners to areas where they would be endangered by the bomb?

The advisory group, including the scientific panel, came to the conclusion that the bomb should be used if no other way could be found to force the Japanese to surrender. But a group of scientists working on the Manhattan Project disagreed strongly enough to circulate the Franck Report mentioned, saying it was inadvisable to use a nuclear bomb in an unannounced attack on Japan. This started more of a furor. Scientists working on the bomb were asked to vote for or against; what they selected depended on how the answers were interpreted because, instead of there being a clear-cut yes or no, there were a number of questions and a number of answer choices.

But there were still questions, after the questionnaire. Why not a demonstration of the power of the bomb? Couldn't one be detonated in the upper atmosphere, or at an announced time over Tokyo Bay, or on an unoccupied island or in the desert before an audience of international officials and selected Japanese government and military officials? These were all possibilities that were discussed and argued about, but the answer was no.

The answer has to be taken in the context of the times. We were at war with Japan. Quite fresh in mind was the Pearl Harbor attack, the Bataan Death March, reports of Japanese maltreatment coming back from escaped or liberated prisoners, the memory of Japanese atrocities in China, and other such factors. All things considered, the negative answer was understandable. It is doubtful whether a demonstration given in an uninhabited area would have been convincing. And, as the military kept pointing out, suppose the demonstration bomb turned out to be a dud? And they had no convincing reason to believe that it wouldn't be a dud.

So no orders were ever issued to stop the use of the atomic bomb. After the Hiroshima mission, President Truman said that it was to spare the Japanese people from utter destruction that the Potsdam proclamation was issued, which had been promptly rejected by their leaders. What more would it take for the Japanese to realize that he was telling nothing but the truth? He had no way of knowing at the time of the convolutions taking place inside the Japanese government, moves that were really death convulsions.

Premier Suzuki called for emergency meetings of the Supreme War Council, the full cabinet, and the *jushin*. The council planned to meet at 10:30 Thursday morning, August 9—the same time at which an American plane, *Bock's Car,* having had its own troubles and delays, would be approaching the Nagasaki area.

On the B-29 everything continued to go wrong. After flying around at 30,000 feet over the rendezvous point, meeting Captain Bock and *The Great Artiste* and seeing no sign of Major Hopkins and the photo plane, Major Sweeney headed *Bock's Car* for the primary target, Kokura. With 600 gallons of useless fuel trapped in the bomb-bay tanks, they couldn't afford to waste more precious gas by waiting. A heavily loaded, reciprocating-engine bomber uses a lot of fuel, even when trying to conserve it, flying in the rare atmosphere six miles above the earth.

Weather reports from Kokura and from the secondary target, Nagasaki, were good. Just to be on the safe side, the navigator, Captain Van Pelt, again checked his routes to Kokura and Nagasaki and plotted a course from Kokura to Nagasaki—the shortest one.

The weather had been reported as good over Kokura. It still held when they arrived; Kokura showed up under spotty clouds. The plane swung into position—the whole purpose of a bomb run is to provide a steady, even, constant-speed platform for the bombardier and the bomb as it leaves the plane. Major Sweeney's crew went into the procedure they had practiced so often that it was now second nature. Only this wasn't practice; this was a real, live bomb, a bomb such as the world had never seen, using a man-made element that had been discovered only five years earlier.

The bomb-bay doors opened, and a steady humming sound swept through the plane, a signal that the bomb was ready to be dropped, a signal that would be stopped only when the bomb was released and broke the circuit, or when the bomb-bay doors closed again. Most of the men put on their special Polaroid glasses, made solely for the purpose of protecting their eyes against the light and rays of an atomic blast. Since the glass was so dark that it shut out almost all light, not all the men could put them on until the bomb had been dropped, but before it was detonated. The bombardier and pilots and flight engineer had to be able to see the bombsight and their instruments. They had fifty-two seconds to protect their eyes after the bomb left the plane; in that time, the plane had to make a sharp diving turn and get as far away from the detonation as possible.

Bombardier Beahan put his left eye to the rubber eyepiece of the Norden (MK-15) bombsight and Kokura began to unreel before him between the clouds. He knew, from his briefing and study, just what it should look like. There was the river and the railroad yard. The aiming point and the huge Kokura arsenal had to be less than twenty seconds away. But the arsenal, which turned out light and heavy weapons for the Japanese Army, never came into sight. A blanket of smoke from a nearby fire covered it. Beahan

swore a little and said, "No drop." Major Sweeney told the
crew they were going to try again.

No one wanted to spend more time than necessary over
Kokura. The heavy industries in the area were fringed with
antiaircraft defenses. In addition, the Japanese, who had
been in the habit of ignoring the regular reconnaissance aircraft, might be suspicious, since Hiroshima, of a very small
flight of high-flying B-29s. It was a quirk of fate that the
smoke from Yawata's steel mills, a few miles away and
bombed a couple of days before, should suddenly swing over
and hide the one place in Kokura they had to be able to see.

Again the plane settled into its bomb run, the bomb-bay
doors open, the "ready" signal humming. Again, Beahan
put his eye to the bombsight. This time he saw something
he hadn't seen before, puffs of smoke as flak exploded below them. He called it out to Sweeney. Again the river
showed up, just where expected. And again, the smoke coming in from the west on a strong wind hid the arsenal from
view. But not the sight of the antiaircraft shells coming up
from below. "No drop," Sweeney said again, and decided
to climb higher in an attempt to throw off the Japanese
gunners.

Jake Beser, monitoring the Japanese radio and radar
wavelengths, started picking up signals at the fighter control
wavelengths. Some of these were ground and some were airborne; the latter were getting stronger. The sounds were
soon confirmed visually by a scanner: "Zeros on the way up.
About ten." Sweeney wasn't worried much about the fighter
planes—he didn't think they could reach the bomber's altitude—but the flak could be adjusted to it.

Bock's Car swung around again and tried another bomb
run from a different angle. It was no more effective than
the others; the smoke blowing across from the earlier Yawata
strike obscured the arsenal. With the flak coming closer, it

was getting hairy up over Kokura. The orders were simple and strict: You have to bomb visually. There didn't seem to be any break in the steady wind blowing in from the west, nor did any seem likely.

Sergeant Kuharek, the flight engineer, reported that the fuel situation was now critical; there was barely enough to get them back to Iwo Jima. Sweeney and Ashworth decided they should head southwest for Nagasaki. Van Pelt said he had already plotted a course, the most direct, even though that would take them over some Kyushu fighter bases.

Major Sweeney made an odd but understandable mistake as he turned away from Kokura toward Nagasaki. Not seeing *The Great Artiste* behind him after he had changed course abruptly, he automatically said, "Where's Bock?" But instead of asking the question on the intercom, he had pressed the open transmission button. Without meaning to, he had broken the long radio silence. Far away, Major Hopkins, still despairingly circling his camera plane over the wrong island off the southern tip of Kyushu, heard the sudden two-word question and immediately answered, "Is that you Chuck? Where the hell are you?" Sweeney, realizing what he had done, quickly closed the open switch. He wasn't going to compound the error. The lost camera plane remained lost.

Major Sweeney had a number of things on his mind now. There was the problem of fuel, there was the fat, lethal bomb hanging from its shackles in the bomb bay, there were the fighter bases over which they'd be flying, and there was Nagasaki. What if it should turn out to be as obscured as Kokura had been?

All kinds of things were going on at Nagasaki, almost none of them connected with atomic bombs. The big industrial port was going about its business on a typically hot August day. Nagasaki's seaport business had declined steadily in the past year as American planes, ships, and mines tightened their slow strangulation of Japan's sea movement. But the industrial plants were still turning out all forms of heavy and light war materials, though shortages had put them far behind their schedules.

Although news of what had happened at Hiroshima was deliberately being kept from the people, there were a few in Nagasaki who knew a certain amount about the results of the atomic bombing there. Among them were the newsmen who worked at the Nagasaki branch of the Domei News Bureau. As communications (along with everything else) gradually broke down under the stress of war and incessant bombing, the radio and wires of Domei were increasingly being used by the military and the government for collecting and passing on both classified and open information, as well as for disseminating to the general public what the government thought it should know.

On August 7, the people at Domei's Nagasaki bureau received a special announcement from Imperial Headquarters that the day before, Hiroshima had been attacked by a small force of B-29s using a new type of bomb that had inflicted heavy damage. The following day, August 8, there had been an additional announcement from Imperial Headquarters, giving further details of the previous statement. This was not intended for the general public, of course. The additional information was more puzzling than helpful, stating merely that the new bomb was dropped by parachute, exploding with a blinding flash five or six hundred yards above the ground and affecting the skin of people exposed on the ground unless they were clothed in white.

This was a mixture of fact and incorrect deductions. It was natural for anyone seeing the parachutes of the instruments dropped by the instrument plane before the detonation to conclude that they had carried the explosives. The bomb had been detonated at about one-thousand feet above the city, or about six-hundred yards. And people far enough away to receive surface burns from the blast were better off if they were wearing heat-reflecting white clothing rather than heat-absorbing colors. There were examples of this on living people, of burns in patterns conforming to the patterns on their clothing. The best example came from open books, far enough away from the detonation not to have been burned up. On open pages, the white paper seemed untouched, but the flash had completely burned out the black letters.

A more puzzling matter for the Nagasaki bureau to unravel was the complete absence of the usually routine damage report from the city—the number of buildings destroyed, the number of casualties, and the like. That question was cleared up at about ten o'clock in the morning of the next day, the ninth, when information came into the Domei office, top secret, not to be passed on to unauthorized personnel. This information revealed that thousands of buildings had been destroyed at Hiroshima, that more than 100,000 people had been killed, and that there were at least that many wounded. Nagasaki and Hiroshima were small cities, with prewar populations of between 250,000 and 350,000; while many civilians had moved out of Hiroshima for various reasons during the war, it had been swollen by the fact that it was headquarters for the Second Imperial Army, selected to defend southern Japan. The first bomb had been detonated eighteen-hundred feet above this Army's headquarters. The Army, in effect, had been destroyed by one bomb, or at least put out of commission. Nagasaki did not have an unusual concentration of military people; it had light and heavy industry, mainly the Mitsubishi factories in two separate complexes—the shipyards and, a few miles away, the arms factory, manufacturing various items ranging from small arms to torpedoes. The wartime movement of population out of Nagasaki was balanced by the move of workers into the area's war plants.

Nagasaki is in a hilly, broken-up area. The name means "long valley"; actually it is more like two valleys in the shape of an irregular X with the lower legs practically cut off and the upper ones mismatched. The right-hand valley and the center of the X is the old city, with the harbor at the base. The left-hand, and much longer, valley is called Urakami. The valleys are separated, as they diverge, by hills, some as high as twelve to thirteen hundred feet. Since there are other hills beyond the valleys, living and working space is concentrated in certain areas. The main street of the left-hand, northwest valley is Urakami Street, and along it, to the left, runs the Urakami River.

As *Bock's Car* approached Nagasaki, its bad luck continued. The two-tenths cloud cover of the weather plane's report three hours earlier had changed to about nine-tenths cover. The fuel situation had become desperate. Flight Engineer Kuharek had been checking and rechecking his figures. He told Sweeney that at the best there would be enough fuel for one bomb run over Nagasaki and then, with luck, to get them to Okinawa. There was no chance now of returning as far as Iwo without refueling.

Having taken the most direct route from spared Kokura, without response from the fighter bases below, they were approaching Nagasaki from the northeast. And the east wind that brought smoke from Yawata to cover the aiming point at Kokura had brought clouds to cover most of Nagasaki.

The sequence of events that followed, and their accuracy by recall, depends on who is telling the story. The general version is that before they started their bomb run, Sweeney and Ashworth had a quick conference. There was a divided command there, no novelty for the Pacific where MacArthur controlled the ground forces and Nimitz, the Navy. Sweeney was the aircraft commander; Ashworth was in charge of the bomb.

Sweeney explained the fuel situation to Ashworth. The cloud cover made visual bombing unlikely if not impossible. But their instructions were to bomb visually only. Sweeney said they could be accurate to within a thousand feet bombing by radar. Ashworth considered the alternatives and consequences. He had been a part of the Manhattan Project almost since its inception, he had selected the Tinian site, he had been the one to tell Admiral Nimitz about the bomb. As assistant to "Deak" Parsons, Dr. Oppenheimer's deputy, he knew as much about the overall situation and the inner workings of the bomb as any military man.

He asked for a little time to think over the question. If the cloud cover didn't open up at all, either they'd have to bomb by radar, which had been forbidden, or they wouldn't use the bomb at all on this trip. If they didn't use it, they would have to ditch it at sea or try to get it back to Okinawa. If they decided on the latter, the extra five tons might make it impossible for them to reach that emergency goal. And if they reached the air base at Okinawa, how would the bomb react to even the smoothest landing, much less to a possible rough one? Suppose it should be detonated on landing, not only blowing up the plane but the Yontan air base and a large piece of the island with its civilian population and American military personnel and equipment? Ashworth knew the thinking behind the use of two bombs —the one–two punch, the use of the second bomb as the convincer. The idea of wasting the plutonium bomb by dumping it into the sea seemed to be throwing away a tremendous amount of planning and the work of thousands of people, not to mention millions of dollars.

He made up his mind. "Drop it by radar if you can't do it visually," he said. "I'll take the responsibility."

The aiming point was the Mitsubishi shipyards. The

bomb was supposed to be detonated just slightly below and to the right of the bottom of the X at the edge of the harbor. In that way it would demolish the industrial heart of the city and the port. The level ground there would give it the greatest range for damage to property. The navigator, Captain Van Pelt, and the radarman, Sergeant Buckley, concentrated on their scopes, trying to bring the plane to the proper dropping point before releasing the bomb. They were about half a minute away.

Suddenly there was a slight break in the clouds. Kermit Beahan, the bombardier, saw it and spoke up. "I've got it. I'll take it now," he said, and did.

The bomb-bay doors opened. For the fourth time that day, the preliminary humming started. In the bombsight's cross hairs, Beahan had the Mitsubishi Arms Manufacturing Plant, the secondary target. The automatic process started; abruptly the humming stopped and the plane jumped up, suddenly freed of the bomb's weight.

Beahan called out the traditional "Bombs away," and then, realizing this was not properly descriptive, amended it to "Bomb away." Sweeney swung the plane into the sharp diving turn practiced so often by the 509th's bombers. It was 12:02 Tinian time; 11:02 Nagasaki time.

Behind them, Captain Bock and *The Great Artiste* released the clusters of instruments and their parachutes and executed a similar turn in the reverse direction. Attached to each of the three instrument tubes was a copy of a letter addressed to Prof. Ryukochi Sagane. Each letter was the same. Three of the nuclear scientists on Tinian, Dr. Luis Alvarez, Dr. Philip Morrison, and Dr. Ralph Serber, had studied with Dr. Sagane at the University of California in 1938. Knowing that Dr. Sagane, a physicist, was a nuclear expert, they thought he would be able to explain to his government what had happened at Hiroshima, and now at Nagasaki, if they could get through to him.

Headquarters
Atomic Bomb Command
August 9, 1945

TO: PROF. R. SAGANE:

FROM: Three of your former scientific colleagues
during your stay in the United States

We are sending this as a personal message to urge you to use your influence as a reputable nuclear physicist to convince the Japanese General Staff of the terrible consequences which will be suffered by your people if you continue the war.

You have known for several years that an atomic bomb could be built if a nation were willing to pay the enormous cost of preparing the necessary material. Now you have seen that we have constructed the production plants, there can be no doubt in your mind that all the output of these factories, working twenty-four hours a day, will be exploded on your homeland.

Within the space of three weeks, we have proof-fired one bomb in the American desert, exploded one in Hiroshima, and fired a third this morning.

We implore you to confirm these facts to your leaders and to do your utmost to stop the destruction and waste of life which can result in the total annihilation of your cities if continued. As scientists, we deplore the use to which a beautiful discovery has been put, but we can assure you that unless Japan surrenders at once, this rain of atomic bombs will increase many fold in fury.

The letter was unsigned. One of the copies was found in a field about fifteen miles from Nagasaki and taken into the laboratory of an aircraft plant there, eventually opened by an executive who didn't know whether it was another bomb or not. Someone at the plant knew that Dr. Sagane was a physics professor at the University of Tokyo. By the time they reached him and he was able to come pick up the letter, the war was over.

Gravity pulled the bomb from the bomb bay as its restraining shackles were released, setting in motion a series

of predetermined activities aimed at achieving one thing—
the most destructive single explosion man had ever set off.
When the arming wires pulled out of the metal casing, the
bomb's internal machinery started operating on its own internal power. Timing devices held switches open for several
seconds so that no miscalculation or error could detonate
the bomb while it was still close enough to the aircraft to
damage it or its occupants. Barometric fuses closed sequen-
tial switches as the air pressure increased as the bomb fell.
And then the radar proximity fuses closed the final switches
as the radio messages bounced back from the earth while
the falling piece of metal plummeted to within 1,540 feet
of earth.

The closing of the final switches sent a surge of electric
power that had been built up in condensers to a series of
detonators attached to a sensitive explosive. These were the
sixty-three lens molds whose creation had caused such problems at Los Alamos. These, encircling the small sphere of
plutonium, created an implosion, forcing the radioactive material inside to condense into a smaller mass. At the same
time, this action pressed in on a tiny initiator made up of
beryllium and polonium. The polonium sent out alpha rays
which acted on the beryllium, which in turn spewed neutrons out into the two hemispheres of plutonium surrounding it. The plutonium chain reaction probably would have
taken place, and just as quickly, without the initiator. It
was a form of insurance.

Once the fuses were closed, this whole action took place in
a fraction of a second. An amazing amount of energy was
released in a millisecond, affecting the surrounding area
with an unparalleled blast of heat, gamma rays, and a pressure wave that could, and did, crush everything close to it.

The wave hit the two B-29s, now one-thousand feet lower
than they had been when the bomb had been released and
eight miles from the point at which the bomb had been

detonated. The men expected one large shock wave, as at Hiroshima, followed by a less severe "echo" as the original one bounced off the earth's surface back to them. The *Bock's Car* crew had been through it all at Hiroshima in *The Great Artiste*. Captain Bock's crew in the instrument plane had been thoroughly briefed. They all thought they knew what to expect. They had also been told that this was a more efficient type of atomic bomb, so that perhaps the effect would be greater.

Because of the sighting difficulties, the bomb was not detonated over the relatively flat area surrounding the harbor and old city just below the cross of the X, but about two-and-a-half miles to the northwest, up the Urakami Valley, the top left arm of the X. To their surprise, the crews felt five distinct shocks rather than one or two, none of them as violent as expected. Later it was figured that the difference in the intensity of the shock waves resulted from the fact that the bomb had been detonated up the valley, where there was no large clear space but a series of ridges and that the several waves came from the shock waves bouncing off the hills and ridges.

This type of topography limited the damage and destruction in Nagasaki in comparison with that of the less efficient bomb used at Hiroshima. But where the effects were felt, they were, of course, at least as severe. Estimates of the number of deaths at Hiroshima vary from eighty thousand to over two hundred thousand; at Nagasaki, from thirty-nine thousand to seventy-four thousand.

Nagasaki officially had about 90,000 people less than Hiroshima, 252,000 to 344,000, but since these events took place in wartime, no one can be quite sure of the population of each city at the time. There is also a strong suspicion that the number of fatalities at Hiroshima, for instance, was grossly underestimated by the Japanese government. For one thing, the government did not want to admit to the world and to its own people how badly it had been hurt by these new bombs. These events took place at the confusing end of a long and costly war. The almost total destruction of the administrative center of Hiroshima, as well as of its personnel, knocked out any ideas of authoritative statistics. The United States government accepted the figures put out by the Japanese, but some American officials on the scene soon afterwards believe the figures did not include the Japanese military men killed at Hiroshima. The bomb had been detonated directly above Second Army Headquarters; no one nearby survived.

CHAPTER V

In the Palace
Air-Raid Shelter

When the bomb went off over Nagasaki, there were a few people who recognized it immediately for what it was—an atomic blast. They were those who had been in Hiroshima three days earlier. The amazing flash of light was enough to make anyone who had survived the first one duck for cover at once. The survivors had learned a few things from experience—there are reports from the few who happened to be in both cities at the time and survived. They had learned that they had to be protected from the direct effects of the radiant heat or they would be burned to death, protected either by distance or by something material between them and the source of the heat.

They had also learned that they had to be away from windows—the injury to people caused by flying broken glass was tremendous. They had to be protected from buildings falling from the tremendous pressure change. They didn't realize then that they had to be protected from radiation, but protection from the immediate heat generally served the same purpose. The fires would come later.

No one who was near the epicenter was able to describe

the blast because no one who could see it close up survived. Beneath the point of detonation was a circle with a radius of about one thousand yards in which everything living without heavy shielding was incinerated. Viewers farther away remember only the blinding flash of light. As at Hiroshima, almost no one who was fairly close commented on any noise. It is possible that the noise from the pressure wave was so intense that the pressure itself immobilized the ears, perhaps stunning the eardrums, or that the sound was too large for the senses to pass it on or take it in. People much farther away reported hearing a tremendous roar.

Following the blast, a huge fireball formed, taking up the space between the ridges in the Urakami Valley and spreading over the tops of hills and over the next valleys. Soon afterwards, the now-familiar mushroom cloud formed and started rising thousands of feet into the air, bringing with it dirt and debris from the smashed buildings below.

Nagasaki was not only the locale for Lieutenant Pinkerton and *Madame Butterfly*, it was also the center of Catholicism in Japan, Kyushu having been visited by S. Francis Xavier in 1549. In commemoration of this visit, in the nineteenth century, after the religious persecution had stopped, the parishioners had built Our Lady of the Immaculate Conception, the largest Roman Catholic cathedral in the Orient. It was on the eastern side of the valley, nearly a thousand yards from the epicenter, and at 11 A.M. on August 9, 1945, several hundred members of its congregation were gathered there. At 11:02, the roof, along with various pieces of masonry, fell in on them, killing them all. It was an American, Commodore Matthew Calbraith Perry, who opened Japan to the West, which eventually brought about changes making a Western religion such as Catholicism legal; it was an American bomb that killed more Japanese Catholics (seven thousand) than the most violent religious persecution there.

All over Nagasaki, the pattern of Hiroshima was being repeated, though on a smaller scale. Not as far as the individuals were concerned, because there the scale is personal—one's own death, one's own pain, the death or suffering of someone near or dear, is the only reality anyone can take in at the time. It is not made any better or worse, for each individual, by the fact that there are a thousand of them as against a hundred or a hundred thousand.

Survivors thought the bomb must have gone off directly above them or very close to them. They could not take in the idea of a blast so great that its effect at a distance was as though it had been detonated close to them. And there were the same kinds of freaks of fate: groups of people and buildings the same distance from the epicenter were wiped out or spared or only slightly damaged depending on what seemed to be chance but were really accidents of nature, the intervention of a small hill or a change in topography that mitigated the effect of the heat, pressure, or radiation.

And, as at Hiroshima, the people who were still able to move tried to get out, to get away to anywhere except where they were. Any place else must be better. Most of the city's services were cut off: water didn't flow because too many mains were broken, surface vehicles that were in the Urakami Valley area were burned up, those from far away couldn't get through the disrupted, torn-up, blocked-off streets. But the factors that made Urakami a valley, the surrounding hills and ridges, cut short the spread of radiation and blast and heat, leaving the adjacent countryside less affected than at Hiroshima, leaving untouched or undamaged more and closer havens of help.

Bock's Car and *The Great Artiste*, having survived the shock waves, turned and went back to check on the damage, taking pictures. As was the case with the men over Hiroshima, they were amazed at what they saw, although except for Commander Ashworth, Lieutenant Barnes, and Captain

Olivi, the men on the strike plane had been aboard the instrument plane at the earlier detonation. The sight, even from six miles up, of the sudden death of a large portion of a city is one that cannot be believed even when seen.

The planes did not stay long over Nagasaki. The strike plane didn't have fuel to waste on sightseeing, even at the most awesome of sights. They turned south-southwest and started down the Osimi and Ryukyu islands for the big air base at Okinawa. Less than half an hour after they left, Major Hopkins' photographic plane, attracted by the blast, flew over the stricken city and followed the others to Okinawa. Abe Spitzer, the radioman for the strike plane, sent out a message for headquarters at Tinian, reporting that Nagasaki had been bombed visually with no fighter opposition and no flak, that visible effects were about the same as at Hiroshima, and that they were heading for Okinawa as there was only enough fuel to get there.

The latter was more a hope than a fact. Radio messages to the Air–Sea rescue units were not answered, although Sweeney wanted to warn them of the possibility of having to ditch. The Air–Sea units, knowing nothing of the delays over Yakashima and Kokura, assumed that the original target had been bombed and that the planes were heading back to Tinian; they, too, had gone home. As it neared Okinawa, with fuel gauges hovering at the Empty, *Bock's Car* tried to radio Yontan Field, but got no response. Sweeney wanted to let them know that a plane was going to land there that was not only unexpected but that didn't have enough fuel to wait for clearance.

As they got within sight of the field, the situation looked impossible. What seemed like hordes of fighters and bombers were taking off and landing. Repeated calls to the tower at Yontan got no answers. Sweeney headed down the long runway so that they could come down, ready or no, in case their fuel supply ran out competely.

It was obvious that radio calls weren't getting through to Yontan, or anywhere else on Okinawa, so Sweeney ordered flares set off, which also got no attention. In frustration and desperation, he ordered every flare on the plane to be shot off. They were, practically, a rainbow of signals, telling those who could translate them that a plane was coming in for a landing with all kinds of problems: out of fuel, dead and wounded on board, aircraft on fire, etc. This move, at any rate, got attention. Planes moved away from the runway like chickens scattering from a hawk.

Sweeney brought *Bock's Car* down sharply, hit around the middle of the runway going faster than normal for a landing, bounced once, and settled down. The reversible propellers brought it to a halt before they ran out of concrete, crash wagons came up alongside to take care of the dead and wounded and to put out the fire, and a jeep showed up to haul the plane to a hard stand.

When a ground crew man poked his head in to ask where the dead and wounded were, Sweeney reportedly signaled with a thumb extended northeast, toward Nagasaki, and said, "Back there."

Moments later, Fred Bock brought his plane in near them, and much after that, Major Hopkins and the missing camera plane showed up. Major Sweeney and Commander Ashworth got in touch with Gen. Jimmy Doolittle, in charge of the Eighth Air Force on Okinawa, and told him the story of the mission. Commander Ashworth reported in some detail to the command base at Tinian. After refueling, the planes took off for the long return trip to Tinian, arriving there at 2225 (10:25 P.M.), nineteen hours and forty minutes after they took off, all but two of which had been spent in the air.

Back in Nagasaki, conditions had gone from bad to worse. About an hour after the strike, while the mushroom cloud, extending to a height of twelve miles or more, was still hanging over the city, a black rain started to fall. The same thing

had happened at Hiroshima. It was a condensation caused
by the cooler upper air acting on the moisture sucked up
from the bay and the ground by the giant fireball. The color
was dark because the moisture had to pass through the debris
and dust and burning particles and ash that made up much
of the cloud. The rain to a certain extent prevented the fires
that had been started from spreading any farther.

At about the same time the ruin was setting in on Nagasaki, the Supreme War Council was meeting at Tokyo, the
meeting that had been called for the day before but was postponed. Earlier in the morning, Foreign Minister Togo had
been calling on Premier Suzuki, angrily telling him that
valuable time had been lost by the previous day's postpone-
ment, that there was no time to be wasted, and that a Supreme Council meeting must be called at once. Suzuki rather
surprisingly agreed at once and started for the Palace.

A little before that, Marquis Kido had arrived at the
Palace and discussed with the Emperor the situation as they
knew it at the time—they didn't know then of *Bock's Car* and
its lethal load flying over the home islands, but they knew
that Soviet armies had crossed into Manchuria and were falling on the depleted Kwantung Army like the well-known
wolf on the fold. His Majesty told Kido to get in touch with
the Premier and inform him of the need for immediate action. Suzuki agreed with Kido that the only course that could
be taken at the moment was to recommend immediate acceptance of the Potsdam terms and promised to convene the
Supreme War Council and the cabinet as soon as possible.

Suzuki told the Chief Cabinet Secretary, Hisatsune Sakomizu, "Let our present cabinet take the responsibility of
seeing the country through the termination of the war."
Normally, Suzuki and his cabinet would have been expected
to resign. Their considered policy, continuation of the war
while trying to get the Soviet Union to act as a mediator,
had been a complete failure. But what would have been

enough to topple a government in normal times was not ap-
plicable now. This was Thursday, August 9, 1945. The cabinet knew about the atomic bomb at Hiroshima; in a little
while it would hear about the second one at Nagasaki. There
had to be a government around to make some kind of a surrender offer.

The hard-working and aware Foreign Minister, Shigenori
Togo, knew that. After pressuring Suzuki, Togo went in
search of Admiral Yonai to make sure of his support at the
upcoming meeting. The Navy Minister agreed that their
country had no choice but to sue for peace. While still at the
Navy Ministry, Togo met Imperial Prince Takamatsu, a
Navy captain and the Emperor's second youngest brother,
who asked the Foreign Minister's views on the situation.
Togo answered as well as he could: It was now too late to get
any better terms than those set down in the Potsdam proclamation, although he'd do the best he could.

At 10:30 that morning, as *Bock's Car* was on its way from
Kokura to Nagasaki, the Supreme War Council finally met
again at the Imperial Palace to continue its calm and unhurried deliberations, calm and unhurried not because the
members didn't understand the gravity of the problem, although some of them still thought they had a chance to improve things, but because of the human inability to face un-
pleasant facts, to arrive at undesirable conclusions, and to
make recommendations that seemed unthinkable.

Premier Suzuki opened the meeting with a brief talk, out-
lining the situation. Considering what had happened at
Hiroshima and now the Soviet entry into the war, Japan was
in no position to continue fighting. There was no alternative
to acceptance of the Potsdam terms.

He asked for opinions. And got silence.

Finally, Admiral Yonai broke the spell. "We're not going
to accomplish anything unless we speak out," he said. "Do
we accept the enemy ultimatum unconditionally? Do we pro-

pose conditions? If so, we had better discuss them here and now." That started the discussion.

There was agreement on only one point: The imperial structure must be preserved. Beyond that, chaos. Suzuki, Togo, and Yonai were in favor of accepting the Potsdam conditions, with the imperial polity added. War Minister Anami, Army Chief of Staff Umezu, and Navy Chief of Staff Toyoda spoke up for other conditions. They wanted the size of the occupation force to be limited by the Japanese, the demobilization of the troops to be done on orders from Japanese officers, the trials of war criminals to be conducted by Japan, not the Allies. From their talk it was obvious that they could not accept the idea of defeat or surrender, much less the fact.

While they were arguing, they received word of the detonation over Nagasaki of the second atomic bomb. The debate went on, this latest catastrophe being ignored as much as possible. Anami remained adamant, as though it had not been he who had said just a little earlier, "I am convinced that the Americans have only one bomb."

At that time, Anami, the War Minister, was the most powerful man in Japan, not only because of his position but because of his personality. He was a man noted more for his perseverance than for his brilliance. Wanting to join the Army, he had failed his military examinations four times, but he finally made it. In 1926, he was made Hirohito's military aide. During the 1930s when the military ran wild, he was a middle-of-the-roader. During the days of the military's greatest expansion, he commanded the Army in the Dutch East Indies. He was regarded as an able administrator, and not impervious to reason, which was one of the reasons he had been chosen to be War Minister in Suzuki's cabinet. Since this had to be an end-the-war cabinet, the War Minister had to be both a comparatively reasonable man and someone acceptable to the Army.

Nevertheless, his job was to represent the Army in the cabinet and supercabinet meetings and discussions. So Anami spoke up against any terms that would compromise the position of the Emperor or the Army. Togo said that Japan's position was now such that if she brought up any conditions at all, the Allies might refuse to negotiate. Anami's position was backed, not unexpectedly, by the Army Chief of Staff, Gen. Yoshijiro Umezu, a rigid, gruff, no-nonsense type of soldier, a product of the Kwantung Army who looked like an Oriental Mussolini.

Umezu took the military's position in the debate, saying that Japan had still not lost the war, that the enemy should be forced to invade the home islands at which time the Japanese forces would inflict tremendous losses and perhaps even keep him from landing. Togo answered that even if the first invasion attempt should be repulsed, Japanese ability to defend herself would be further decreased, and a second invasion would certainly succeed. The only thing Japan could do was accept the Potsdam terms at once, asking for no more than that the Imperial House be preserved.

On that note, with no agreement in sight, the council adjourned. It had been in session for two and a half hours; it was still split down the middle, just as it had been before, as though the Soviet entry into the war had not taken place, as though the second atomic bomb had not been dropped on one of its major cities. Premier Suzuki suggested that the council reconvene later in the day when the scheduled afternoon meeting of the full cabinet was over.

The cabinet met at 2:30 that afternoon at the premier's official residence. Togo opened the discussion, telling the ministers what had gone on before the Russian intervention, including Ambassador Sato's attempts to have the Kremlin use its good offices to mediate. For the benefit of those who didn't know about it, he described what had happened at

Hiroshima and repeated the first reports from Nagasaki. Suzuki asked for opinions and was answered, predictably, by the ministers of the Navy and War.

Admiral Yonai agreed with Togo, saying that although Japan might win the first battle, it would lose the second and that as the war was lost, the only sensible course was to surrender. The thing to do now was to consider how best the country might be preserved.

General Anami answered for the hawks, saying that it was too early to say the war was lost, that victory could not be promised but the losses inflicted on an invading force might be so great that the situation might be reversed. He continued with another basic Japanese argument: "Our Army will not submit to demobilization. Our men simply will not lay down their arms. And since they know they are not permitted to surrender, since they know that a fighting man who surrenders is liable to extremely heavy punishment, there is really no alternative for us but to continue the war."

Various ministers objected, pointing out the depleted condition of Japan in all respects—the people were exhausted, the rice crop was the poorest in many years, bombings were growing steadily worse and more effective, the total picture being that the strength and means were no longer available to continue to wage war.

Anami agreed with their estimate of the situation. "But," he said, "we must fight the war through to the end no matter how great the odds against us!"

The Home Minister, Genki Abe, seemed to agree. If the cabinet's way to end the war was by capitulation, he said, he could not promise civil obedience and referred to the uprising of February, 1936, which, with good reason, was very much on everyone's mind.

At that time, a group of junior officers, imbued with a peculiar form of patriotism (they knew best; everyone else in power, Army or government, was corrupt) made a power play that for a short time literally paralyzed the nation. Using the excuse of extreme and total dedication to the Emperor and the mystique of the Emperor's divinity, they seized power, separated the Emperor and his palace from the rest of the country, assassinated, or attempted to assassinate, their enemies—the politicians who denied them their "rights."

They were quite open about what they were trying to do. They wrote a manifesto explaining their motives and saw that copies were delivered early in the morning of February 26, 1936, to the offices of the leading Tokyo newspapers. It was a joint effort, but signed only by two captains of the Third Infantry Regiment, Shiro Nonaka and Teruzo Ando. The manifesto said that the Emperor was the essence of the Japanese nation. Then it said that now was the time to expand Japan's power and prestige. Many people have made wealth their chief objective, regardless of the general welfare or prosperity of the people, and have thus infringed the prerogatives of the Imperial line. "The elder statesmen (*genro*), the financial magnates (*zaibatsu*), the Government officials and the political parties are responsible."

The manifesto continued, discussing the London Naval Agreement limiting the Japanese Navy in comparison with that of Britain and the United States and the earlier assassinations of Premier Hamaguchi and of Army Chief of Staff General Nagata. The manifesto then stated that it was clear that the country was on the verge of war with Russia, China, Britain, and America who wished to crush the homeland. "Therefore it is our duty to take proper steps to safeguard the Fatherland by killing those responsible. . . . We believe it is our duty to remove the villains who surround the Throne." The inflammatory document concluded with assurances that the signers acted with pure sincerity of heart and with requests for assistance from the spirits of their ancestors.

This was formulated and put out less than a week after

general elections for a new Diet in which the die-hard rightists who wanted to emulate the regimes in Germany and Italy had lost ground to more moderate conservatives. On February 26, the day the manifesto appeared in the papers, about fourteen hundred young officers and enlisted men went on a rampage. They occupied the War Ministry and offices of the Army General Staff and stormed the house of the Minister of War, Hayashi. They gave the War Minister their demands and then allowed the man to go to the Imperial Palace and present them to the Emperor. They killed a number of people, including the eighty-year-old Viscount Saito, the Lord Keeper of the Privy Seal; Korekiyo Takahashi, the Finance Minister (because he was suspected of wanting to limit the military budget); and General Jotaro Watanabe of the Army General Staff, along with his wife and servants. Their attempts to kill Admiral Okada, the Premier, were foiled by his brother-in-law, Colonel Matsuo, who, pretending to be the man they were looking for, was shot down forthwith.

When the rebels went after Admiral Suzuki, it was Captain Ando himself who led the raid. Finding the elderly naval hero asleep, Ando awakened him and spent some time explaining why he was being assassinated. Suzuki listened and said, "Is that all you have to tell me? If this is your argument, then shoot." Captain Ando shot him, once in the chest, once in the leg, and once in the head, and held a dagger to deliver the *coup de grace*. Mrs. Suzuki, hearing the shots, rushed in, took in the situation, and said that for the sake of her husband's honor, and her family's, if her husband had to die, she should be the one to deliver the final blow. She took the dagger from the stunned Captain Ando, who left immediately with his companions. Suzuki was rushed to the hospital and, after a period of touch-and-go, survived—with memories that never left him.

The plotters had pretty well paralyzed Tokyo, having

taken over the police headquarters as well as the military. They had encircled the Palace, but it was not completely cut off—they "had a little list" and would let through their lines intimates of the Emperor who weren't on their list. But telephone service for the city was stopped, as was all public transportation and almost every activity.

The Emperor was reportedly furious at the actions, theoretically being done in his name. The Navy, which was not officially in on the plot, and two of whose high-ranking members had been killed, was also angry. The Emperor let the top Army brass know how angry he was, and the Navy put ships into Tokyo Bay with landing parties ready for action. The Emperor called the rebels' action a mutiny rather than use their term, *incident,* and said there would be no bargaining with the leaders.

The mutiny ended without the public platform the rebels had expected. The enlisted men were promised amnesty if they returned to their barracks, and over a hundred young officers were arrested, arraigned, and charged with treason. They were tried before a series of secret courts martial. Fifteen were sentenced to death and were quickly put before the firing squads. Captain Ando shot himself before the trial. The Emperor put a stop to their expected public trial to avoid inflammatory speeches and to prevent the rebels from appearing as martyrs. The February twenty-sixth mutiny was over, but its influence lasted, still being felt in August, 1945, nine-and-a-half years later.

When Home Minister Abe said that he could not promise civil obedience, he was referring to the 1936 mutiny as his reason for advising against acceptance of the Potsdam terms. Togo, having relayed to the ministers the results of the morning's Supreme War Council meeting, said he felt the cabinet must accept the Potsdam proclamation, as long as the Imperial stucture remained intact. Two other ministers said they agreed with Anami that Japan should insist on other

conditions. After a brief recess for a meal, the ministers reconvened and debated in the same way until ten o'clock,
when it became obvious that there was no consensus. The
cabinet rule required unanimity; on this uncertain note,
the meeting ended, having lasted, except for an hour for
dinner, for seven and a half hours.

Premier Suzuki was not unprepared for the lack of progress. He had discussed the possibility of a total impasse, and
had come to the conclusion, as had others in the government,
that in such an instance, they would go to the Emperor. With
that in mind, he had asked Cabinet Secretary Sakomizu to
get General Umezu and Admiral Toyoda to sign a petition
which would enable Suzuki to convoke a meeting of the Big
Six in the Imperial presence.

Obtaining these signatures wasn't as difficult as it might
have seemed. The Secretary's excuse was that preparing this
in advance would save time in case a meeting with the Emperor had to be called suddenly. The two military men
signed without a question; because the tradition was that the
government did not approach the Throne with a problem
until the government's own solution was unanimous, they
could see no danger in it. The position of the Japanese Emperor was to approve what had already been decided; he was
not expected to take sides or express opinions.

The people of the United States thought the Emperor of
Japan was the chief of state, the head of the government. The
Japanese saw him as a divine being, the living embodiment
of their god-inspired government. We thought he could take
action, tell people what to do, make policies, and see they
were carried out. If we had not thought so, perhaps we
wouldn't have put up such a fuss about their desire to keep
the system as it was.

Actually, the Emperor of Japan was not supposed to be
disturbed for such small details. It was unthinkable to present him with a divided cabinet. If a cabinet was so divided

that it could not present him with a solution that was unanimous, it would resign. That was the way Japanese governments changed. But these were strange times. Japan was about to lose a war for the first time. This was a unique period in Japanese history and required an action equally unique.

Oddly enough, this unprecedented move had been thought of ahead of time, and even discussed with the Emperor. After the inconclusive and deadlocked meetings of first the Big Six and then the full cabinet, Togo and Suzuki went back to the Palace, where they were not unexpected. The Emperor saw them immediately. They reported the results, or lack of them, of the two earlier meetings that day, and Suzuki suggested that the Supreme War Council be reconvened that night in the presence of the Emperor. Hirohito, who had been expecting such a suggestion, approved immediately.

For some time now, the Japanese people and government had seemed to be living on two different levels. One was the practical world, in which they ate, bathed, dressed, slept, and worried about their real problems which included survival, bombs, and death. The other was an unreal world, in which they talked and talked, lofty words of lofty ideals, as a substitute for action. All of a sudden the mood had shifted. Some of the top men in the government seemed to realize that something had to be done. At once. And if they acted, the people, it was presumed, would follow. The question was, would the Army?

The meeting was scheduled for 11:30 that night, in the basement bomb shelter beneath the Palace grounds. Eleven men were gathered there at that hour, waiting for their Emperor. In addition to the Big Six were some of their aides, Sumihisa Ikeda, the Director of the Overall Planning Bureau; Zenshiro Hoshina, Director of the Bureau of Naval Affairs; and Masao Yoshizumi, Director of the Bureau of Military Affairs. Suzuki had also invited two other men, Chief Cabinet

Secretary Hisatsune Sakomizu and Baron Kiichiro Hiranuma, President of the Privy Council.

The room where these men waited that August night was a hothouse, more suitable for raising tropical plants than for settling affairs of state. It was the Emperor's private air-raid shelter, theoretically a bombproof spot, a room about thirty feet long and eighteen feet wide. The room had wood paneling along the walls, which rose to a height of about six feet where it met the feet, or base, of steel beams forming angular arches supporting the ceiling. The lighting was adequate, but the ventilation was poor.

The men were lined up on small chairs in front of small, cloth-covered tables, five men on one side, six on the other. At one end of the room, near the only door, was an undecorated screen. In front of it was a plain, straight-backed chair, like the others, and a small, unadorned table waiting for the Emperor, as were the eleven men, uncomfortable in the heat and humidity and with the knowledge of what had to be done, hot in their formal morning clothes or military dress uniforms.

At about ten minutes to twelve, the door opened and two more men came in, the Emperor and General Shigeru Hasunuma, his chief aide-de-camp. The Emperor sat in front of the screen behind the small bare desk; Hasunuma took a chair against the side wall, to the Emperor's right, behind the line of six ministers and aides. The men bowed to the Emperor when he entered and sat down again after he was seated, respectfully turning their eyes away from His Majesty.

It was an unprecedented thing he was doing, interfering in affairs of state. He was a shy man who preferred to live in the privacy to which he felt he was entitled. Unlike many other monarchs, he not only wanted to be left alone, he was left alone. There was nothing commanding about his appearance or manner. He was short, slight, forty-four years old at the time, with eyesight so poor that he rarely ap-

peared without his glasses. He was much more interested in
marine biology than in running the empire. But the time
had come for him to make a move.

It looked as though he was the only one who could make
it. The services were so set in their ways, and so sure they
were doing the right thing, that the impasse looked perma-
nent. The opposing sides were frozen into attitudes that
could not be compromised without some unexpected outside
force. The Emperor might be that other force.

Premier Suzuki, whose day since early that morning had
been almost one uninterrupted round of meetings, stood at
the end to the left of the Emperor and opened the meeting
by asking the cabinet secretary to read aloud the Potsdam
proclamation. The Premier then recapped the results of the
day's meetings, as he had previously done for the Monarch,
and apologized for asking for the Emperor's presence at a
meeting when the ministers had not agreed on a course of
conduct. The council was split down the middle, three to
three. The cabinet, which was the only agency authorized
by the constitution to approve of the country's surrender,
was even more divided: six members approved the surrender
as long as the continuity of the Imperial House was guaranteed, three members favored the four conditions Anami had
spoken for, and five members approved of more than the
single condition, but less than the four.

Suzuki asked for a report from the Foreign Minister, and
Togo again gave the arguments for accepting the Potsdam
terms as long as there was some assurance about the Emperor. Suzuki then called on the Navy Minister: Admiral
Yonai said he agreed with the Foreign Minister and sat down
again, his speech delivered.

Anami, of course, jumping to his feet, expressed complete
disagreement. He recapitulated his position: The country
should continue the fight since no battle could be won or lost
until it was fought, and if Japan should be forced to sur-

render, in addition to the continuation of the Imperial structure, she must insist on the right to disarm her own soldiers,
conduct the war trials, and limit the occupation forces.
Anami, not surprisingly, received the complete backing of
General Umezu.

After the Army Chief of Staff spoke, it should have been
the turn of his opposite number, Admiral Toyoda, to speak
for the Navy. But Suzuki pulled a switch, calling on Baron
Hiranuma, instead, whom Suzuki had invited so as to involve
the Privy Council in the matter. Hiranuma, then eighty years
old, was a man whose political outlook had changed with
age. He had been an ultranationalist, an extreme right-
winger. In the period between wars, he had been a leader of
the *Kukohansha,* a rightist organization, and had been among
those responsible for the overthrow of the reform-minded
Wakatsuki cabinet. He had backed General Tanaka for
Premier.

Baron Kiichiro Hiranuma could truly and properly be
called an elder statesman. A man with a long, strong face, in
looks resembling an Oriental Saltonstall from New England,
he was to realize he had been wrong and changed his attitude.
By 1939, when he became Premier, he had dropped many of
his earlier beliefs. He was opposed to the war with the United
States, and worked to reduce the power of the Kwantung
Army. He, too, had survived an assassination attempt. Theoretically, he was present at the deliberations in the bomb
shelter as an observer, but when he started speaking, it was
obvious that he was taking an active role.

He had a sharp and logical mind, and he went after facts
as though they alone could save Japan, or at least enable the
government to make up its mind. He asked what had happened to the attempts to get the Soviet Union to act as
mediators. Why had the Soviet Union declared war on Japan?
It was up to Foreign Minister Togo to answer, and although
he understood the reasoning behind Hiranuma's question-

ing, replying wasn't always simple. The facts about the attempt to use Russia were presented. Togo answered the question about why Russia had declared war on Japan by repeating the Kremlin statement that Japan, by rejecting the Potsdam proclamation, had not demonstrated any peaceable intentions. Hiranuma said that Japan hadn't rejected the proclamation, had they? Togo said no, and Hiranuma asked, "Then why did they say so?" All Togo could answer was, "It's all in their imagination."

This answer may have been an attempt to shield Suzuki from the *mokusatsu* error or it may have been due to the different interpretation nations put on their words and actions when compared to the interpretation of the rest of the world. To everyone but the Japanese, the impression given was that they had rejected the proposals, even though the rejection had not been made formally.

Hiranuma went on with his questioning. Who were the "war criminals" mentioned? Would they have to be turned over to the Allies for trials? Would Japan be allowed to disarm her own troops? Then the elder statesman turned to the conduct of the war, mentioning the Allied mastery of the air and water and seeming ability to raid, by plane or ship, without fear of successful retaliation; the consequent decline in food and armament supplies, followed by the atomic bombing of Hiroshima and Nagasaki; and now the Soviet incursion into Manchuria. In short, could the Army and Navy continue the war; could they protect the home islands?

These last questions were answered by Umezu and Toyoda, but they could not promise victory; all they could do was "exert utmost efforts in the future," which left the lingering question of what they had been doing up to now. Or the concomitant answer that if they had been doing their best, it wasn't good enough in the past nor was there any reason to believe that it would be in the future. Then, picking up Home Minister Abe's line about civil disorder, he asked whether the people's steadfastness might not be undermined by the perilous and depressing conditions facing them if the decision was for an immediate surrender?

By this time, it was nearly 2 A.M., Suzuki answered the last question by saying he felt that if the war were continued, there might be great difficulty in maintaining internal order. Hiranuma realized that he had spoken long enough; he had cleared the air and presented the group, not with a choice, but with the fact that there was no choice for them to make. He summed up the situation, and stopped.

At this point, Suzuki dropped his bomb, one for which most members of the little group were totally unprepared. Rising to speak, he pointed out the obvious—that once again, no agreement had been reached. With that in mind, and considering the urgency of the situation, there seemed to be only one thing to do. Turning to his right, away from the row of ministers and their aides, and toward the head of the room, he said: "Your Imperial Majesty's decision is requested as to which proposal should be adopted, the Foreign Minister's or the one with the four conditions."

The Emperor arose with no hesitation, which was not surprising since the reason the meeting had been called was to use the prestige of the Emperor to break the deadlock in the cabinet and council. What was surprising was that he should speak at all, that he would be asked to make such a decision.

Hirohito was not a trained speaker, his voice, which was somewhat harsh and abrasive, was not strong. He was well aware of the importance of the occasion, and he was nervous. His first few words and sentences were difficult to hear and understand, but as he went on, he gained in confidence. He said that continuation of the war would mean destruction for the nation and a prolongation of bloodshed. He reviewed promises made by the military for defenses which were not ready when promised, some of which would never be available, and added: "I do not believe that the difference between what is and should be can be rectified."

He went on, obviously emotionally upset, to tell of his sorrow at the thought of the people who had served their country so loyally, the soldiers and sailors killed or wounded overseas, the families who had lost their homes and often their lives in air raids at home. He ended with a statement of direction:

"I need not tell you how unbearable I find it to see the brave and loyal fighting men of Japan disarmed. It is equally unbearable that others who have given me devoted service should be threatened with punishment as the instigators of the war. Nevertheless, the time has come when we must bear the unbearable. When I recall the feelings of my Imperial Grandsire, the Emperor Meiji, at the time of the Triple Intervention* I swallow my tears and give my sanction to the proposal to accept the Allied proclamation on the basis outlined by the Foreign Minister."

The men in the room rose automatically, bowing toward the Emperor as he turned and went through the door of the air-raid shelter. Suzuki, the Premier, broke the silence that followed the Emperor's departure: "His Majesty's decision ought to be made the decision of this conference as well." No one contradicted him. In fact, no one said a word.

To put the Emperor's will into practical action, the cabinet had to act. So the council left the Palace grounds and went to the official residence of the Prime Minister where the cabinet ministers were waiting. Word of what had occurred at the council meeting was handed on to them, and there was no debate, no question of what to do—the Emperor had spoken—only a question of the wording of the note of surrender. By four in the morning of August 10, the wording had

---

* The Triple Intervention refers to the time when pressure was exerted on Japan, in 1895, by Russia, Germany, and France, causing her to cede to China the Liaotung Peninsula which she had taken from China in the 1894-95 war.

been agreed upon, and by seven, cables had been sent to Switzerland and Sweden to be sent on to the Allies. The Japanese minister in Sweden was instructed to send the message on to the governments of Great Britain and the Soviet Union through the Swedish government; in similar fashion, the Swiss government would transmit the message to the governments of the United States and China.

The problem in Tokyo early in the morning of August 10, now that the Emperor had spoken, was how to word the message, so that the meaning got through clearly without hurting sensitive and delicate military and ultra-patriotic feelings.

The note, forwarded to Secretary of State James F. Byrnes that day, was signed by Grassli, Chargé d'Affaires ad interim of Switzerland, and started in the usual formal fashion: "I have the honor to inform you that the Japanese Minister to Switzerland, upon instructions received from his government, has requested the Swiss Political Department to advise the Government of the United States of Ameica of the following. . . ."

Following were a few hundred words, the essence of which was: "The Japanese Government are ready to accept the terms enumerated in the joint declaration which was issued at Potsdam on July 26, 1945 . . . with the understanding that the said declaration does not comprise any demand which prejudices the prerogatives of His Majesty as a Sovereign Ruler." Included in the surrender offer was the request that the government of the United States forward its answer through Switzerland.

This was, in effect, the end of the war. Or was it? There were two crucial questions unanswered: How did the line about prerogatives of His Majesty fit in with the declared aim of unconditional surrender? And would the Young Turks in the Japanese military, so long accustomed to getting their own way, accept the surrender?

Wording the phrase about the Emperor had been a subject of debate in the wee hours of the morning. Originally it had read "with the understanding that the said declaration does not include any demand for a change in the status of His Majesty under the national laws." Baron Hiranuma, not liking the phrase, had substituted his own, mentioning the prerogatives as a Sovereign Ruler, using an argument perfectly logical to his traditional mind: The nation and the Emperor were one and the same, having existed simultaneously since the beginning.

Semantics had raised its head again. Baron Hiranuma insisted on the word *taiken*, which means "power inherent in the crown." Toshikazu Kase, the Foreign Office Secretary, who translated the note into English, said that after some thought, he decided to translate the word as "prerogatives."

Some of the cabinet and council thought they had ended the war early in the morning by accepting the Emperor's dictum to accept the Potsdam terms. But during the morning of August 10, hundreds of American B-29s and Navy planes showered Tokyo with incendiary bombs, while other Allied aircraft hit many more Japanese cities.

CHAPTER VI

The Pot Boils Furiously

During the council meeting, General Anami had asked
Suzuki what would be done if the enemy gave no assurance
that the Imperial House would be preserved: "Will you go
on fighting?"

Suzuki had looked at him for a moment and answered
quietly, "Yes, we will continue the war." Anami asked
Admiral Yonai the same question and received the same
answer.

Now, in the cold light of day, the general had to tell his
men what had happened. Having called all personnel above
chief-of-section rank to gather in the Ministry's bomb shelter
at 9:30, he gave them a quick review of the activities of the
past few days, including mention of the cables sent to
Switzerland and Sweden. The news, though it couldn't have
been completely unexpected by the more knowledgeable of
the younger officers, seemed to stun them into silence. As is
often the case, though their minds had warned them of the
possibility of such an action, their emotions were unwilling
to accept the facts. They had lost, the unthinkable had taken
place, their world, as they knew it, would never be the same.

No longer would they rule Japan. The question became: Would there still be an Army? Would there still be a Japan?

It was obvious to General Anami that despite their talk of loyalty to the Emperor above all, many of them believed that they knew better than the semisacred object of their worship, that he must have been led astray by the usual traitorous or corrupt advisers. General Anami was a thorough Army man, trained in its ways and approving of them. He was also a loyal man, to his nation and to his Emperor, and he was not stupid. He had been there, at the meetings. He knew, better than most of the younger officers, what the actual war-waging potential of the country was; he was not as blinded to the facts by emotion. Besides, the Emperor had spoken.

He told them again, explaining that there was no choice, no alternative, that they had to abide by the Emperor's decision. He reminded them that they were soldiers. He told them that they were waiting now for the enemy's answer to the note that had been sent, but no matter how it was answered, they, the fighting men of Japan, had to obey orders. In this crisis the uncontrolled actions of one man could bring disaster to the country. One of the young officers asked whether the War Minister was actually considering surrender.

Anami was capable of the dramatic gesture when needed. He cracked his swagger stick down on the table so that it rang like a shot and said, "Anyone who isn't willing to obey my orders will have to do so over my dead body."

What followed was a series of confusions about how to handle developments and news of developments, in Washington and in Tokyo. In Tokyo, the debate was whether and how to let the people know what the high government officials knew—that Japan, with a reservation, had accepted the Potsdam proclamation. This question was to remain for some time, even after the matter of keeping it quiet might have become a theoretical matter. At a time when high officials on all sides were in a state of nervous tension brought on by the long war and its obviously approaching end, when days and hours and moments seemed precious, the delays due to the gap in time between generally accurate but unofficial news broadcasts and the official diplomatic messages were unbearable.

Because of the difference in time zones, the Japanese acceptance was received in Washington at nearly the same time, by the clock, as it had left Tokyo. As a result of the thirteen-hour time differential and the international date line, at about 10 A.M. Friday, August 10, while General Anami was trying to lay down the law to his obedient and rebellious officers and aides, President Truman was meeting at the White House with Secretary of State Byrnes and other key advisers. The message had been received late at night but not passed on until early morning.

The Japanese, who had had trouble deciding whether to accept the Potsdam proclamation and then more trouble drafting the message that would accept the terms in principle, would have been surprised to witness the trouble their acceptance caused in Washington. All the problems in Washington, and many of those in Tokyo, got down to one dilemma: How could conditions about the future status of an individual, the Emperor, be reconciled with the phrase *unconditional surrender*? Again a semantic question. The Japanese, after much argument, had thrown in the phrase about not prejudicing the prerogatives of His Majesty as a Sovereign Ruler.

Admiral Leahy, the President's chief military adviser, urged prompt acceptance, so as to stop the war and bloodshed at once. Leahy had not understood the concept of the atomic bomb, nor had he believed it would work. But now, he didn't see any point in quibbling about small points; to him the issue was clear: Since the Japanese government had accepted the terms, we should get about the task of changing the state of war to one of peace.

Secretary Byrnes didn't see it quite that way. He said, "I do not see why we should retreat from our demand for unconditional surrender. That demand was presented to Japan before the use of the bomb and before the Soviet Union was a belligerent. If any conditions are to be accepted, I want the United States and not Japan to state the conditions."

Just as there were two schools of thought in Tokyo about whether or not Japan should surrender, in Washington there were two schools as to the future role of the Emperor and the Imperial family. There were several reasons for this. One was based on a misinterpretation of the role of the Emperor and Imperial family. Too many of our policymakers, knowing how he was revered, regarded him as a political figure. Another group was caught, like the Japanese military, in the trap of their own words. Since the Japanese military had not acknowledged defeats, how could they now tell the people the war had been lost? In similar fashion, how could men who had threatened the Emperor with a variety of dire fates and indignities suddenly agree to his continuation on the throne?

This battle had been going on for some time in Washington, and positions solidified for each side as they began to believe their own words. But this was only an argument, a discussion, because the end of the war seemed far off. The situation had changed much faster than man's mind could adjust to new facts. The arguments remained as they had been, but the atomic bombs and the entry of Russia into the war had taken these arguments out of the theoretical category and placed them into the front line of practical, immediate issues.

This became a matter of "face" as well as of practical political necessity along with conscience and conviction. How could those Americans who blamed the Emperor for being the chief of the Japanese warmongers who had led their nation down the garden path and forced the United States into a long and bloody war suddenly switch positions without being considered appeasers? The other side said these positions were just names, words, that the Emperor was needed to assure some sort of stability to a beaten nation.

Suddenly, there was no more time for argument; it was a matter for immediate decision. If the Japanese note was accepted in its present form, it would mean that the victorious Allies were allowing the beaten enemy to make conditions, which might affect the future of our relations with the Japanese people and government. If on the other hand, we turned down the note, it might encourage the Japanese to fight on, make a bloody invasion necessary, and add months and untold casualties to a list that was already too long. And if we should reject the note, the American people, tired of a long war, might ask why they should keep on fighting and dying because diplomats and politicians couldn't agree on terms.

Secretary of State Byrnes started working on a reply. It said, after a suitable diplomatic opening and discussion of other matters:

From the moment of surrender, the authority of the Emperor and the Japanese Government to rule the state shall be subject to the Supreme Commander of the Allied powers who will take such steps as he deems proper to effectuate the surrender terms.

The Emperor and Japanese High Command will be required to sign the surrender terms necessary to carry out the provisions of the Potsdam Declaration, and shall issue his own commands to all Japanese military naval and air authorities and to all the forces under their control wherever located to cease active operations and to surrender their arms and to issue such other orders as the Supreme Commander may require to give effect to the surrender terms.

Immediately upon the surrender, the Japanese Government shall transport prisoners of war and civilian internees to places of safety, as directed, where they can be placed aboard Allied transports.

The ultimate form of government of Japan shall, in accordance with the Potsdam Declaration, be established by the freely expressed will of the Japanese people.

The armed forces of the Allied Powers will remain in Japan until the purposes set forth in the Potsdam Proclamation are achieved.

This answer was a good diplomatic effort. It did not say that the Emperor's prerogatives would be abridged, only that they would be subject to the Allied Supreme Commander. By its own terms and words, it acknowledged that the Imperial dynasty would continue without condoning it.

The Secretary of State showed his draft to President Truman, who approved, and then to Secretary of War Stimson, who also approved. Mr. Byrnes had to be very careful with what he said, as he was not only answering for his country but for the other Allies as well. He wanted to answer in such a way that without backing down for the United States, the Japanese would have no reasonable grounds to refuse the terms, and at the same time, the other Allies would have no reason to feel that he had changed any important terms to which they had all previously agreed.

The draft reply was sent out at once for immediate consideration to London, Moscow, and Chungking. Chungking answered approvingly. London requested one change, having to do with the Emperor's signature to the surrender terms. London, which said this might be considered objectionable, approved the draft after this section was changed to "The Emperor will be required to authorize and ensure the signature by the Government of Japan and Japanese Imperial Headquarters of the surrender terms necessary. . . ."

In Moscow, Foreign Commissar Molotov was meeting with

Ambassador Harriman and British Ambassador Clark-Kerr and discussing the Japanese overture. Molotov said that Togo had told Soviet Ambassador Malik that Japan would accept the Potsdam terms so long as the position of the Emperor was not threatened. Molotov, like Byrnes, did not see this as accepting unconditional surrender. While they were talking, George Kennan arrived from the American embassy, bearing the Byrnes note that had just arrived from Washington.

Commissar Molotov looked over the answer and dropped his former frankness, saying his government would have to consider it and would give its answer the next day. Harriman said that time was too important, that he would have to send an answer to Washington that night. Molotov said he'd see what he could do.

The first answer from the Russians got nowhere. Molotov said his government would like to see two Supreme Commanders; one Russian, one American. Harriman, who did not know at the time that Truman had decided to go ahead with the note if the Russians demurred or delayed too long, told Molotov that his condition was "absolutely inadmissible." At two in the morning, Molotov sent for Harriman and Clark-Kerr to let them know that his government agreed to the Byrnes note. Harriman cabled this to Washington at once.

By the time the Allied answers were received, it was August 11. In accordance with Japanese requests, the Byrnes note was given to Max Grassli, the Swiss diplomat in Washington, who informed his government immediately so that they could notify the Japanese government accordingly. The text of the Byrnes note was also released to the American press and radio, making it possible for the Japanese government to get the gist of the reply almost a full day before the slower and more roundabout diplomatic route gave the Japanese the official text of the message. Army and Navy

Secretaries Stimson and Forrestal recommended that all American bombing stop as of that moment, but President Truman overruled them on the theory that this might encourage the Japanese to try more negotiations.

When the note was released to the American press, as figured, it was put on the air as soon as possible. The Japanese Foreign Office monitored a San Francisco radio broadcast of the text a few minutes after midnight of August 12, and Domei picked up another broadcast of the text a few minutes later. This gave the Japanese leaders something to go on, a reply even though still unofficial.

Despite the Emperor's unprecedented action, and the slightly qualified acceptance of the Potsdam terms, the battle of the leaders was still going on. And the Japanese people were learning more of what had been happening, almost accidentally.

On Friday, August 10, the day after the Nagasaki bombing, and after the note accepting the Potsdam terms had been sent out, the morning papers brought the news of the Soviet entry into Manchuria, along with their declaration of war. This included the statement saying that there was no longer any basis to the Japanese government's proposal to the Soviet Union to mediate the war, which was the first the public had heard of the unsuccessful attempts to use the Russians as intermediaries. But, because that one bit of information had been given out, didn't mean that the Army or the government believed the Japanese people should be let in on any more of the truth.

The *jushin* met to consider what else should be told to the people, and so did the cabinet, which had the power to do something about it. There were the usual arguments about the dangers of telling the truth, or even saying anything. The Army was so accustomed to telling the people, and often even their government officials, only what the militarists felt it would be good for them to know that now that some truths had to come out, they didn't know how to go about it. So they argued against doing anything. The Army had never admitted to anything except victories; no moves were made, even backward ones, that were not part of a gigantic, and of course winning, master plan.

The government was not at all sure how the people would react to hearing that the war, for which they had suffered so much, had been lost. The Army had the same fears, and in addition, the shame of having to announce, suddenly, the loss of a war that they had been saying they were winning.

The arguments went both ways. If an immediate announcement of the acceptance of the Potsdam terms were made, it would give the people information and point out the direction they would be taking, thus perhaps minimizing its destructive effects. But if the reply to the note of August 10 did not guarantee the continuation of the power of the Imperial family, it could not be accepted; in that case, the people and fighting forces, knowing that a surrender offer had been made, might lose their enthusiasm to continue the fight.

The final decision was to say nothing, to delay, to wait until there was an answer from the Allies, but to prepare the Japanese people for the news. The Director of the Information Bureau was told to prepare a statement that would meet the situation—nothing more than a hint that an important announcement might be made soon by the government. Hiroshi Shimomura, as Director of the Cabinet's Information Bureau, had the announcement drawn up and went over it carefully with Togo, General Anami, and Admiral Yonai; he then had it transmitted to the radio stations for inclusion in the afternoon news.

The statement went through the usual official euphemisms, praising the spirit and efforts of the fighting men and populace, and then got into grimmer matters. The enemy was preparing to invade Japan, had used the new type of bomb to spread unprecedented death and destruction, and had been joined by the Soviet forces. It ended with two sentences meant to point out that more was to come: "In truth, we cannot but recognize that we are now beset with the worst possible situation. Just as the government is exerting its utmost efforts to defend the homeland, safeguard the polity, and preserve the honor of the nation, so too must the people rise to the occasion and overcome all difficulties in order to protect the polity of their Empire."

While this may have been meant to prepare the people for the forthcoming end of the war on the basis of the Potsdam terms, it also gave the impression of asking for more sacrifices for a last stand against the enemy.

General Anami had gone over the message with Shimomura. The Information Bureau head said that the War Minister had worked hard and conscientiously to shape the statement in accordance with the wishes of the cabinet so as to lessen the shock to the nation when the truth came out. But when the announcement was released, another one was put out, under General Anami's name, that had a completely different meaning. The way in which that was accomplished should have served as a warning for other events.

When General Anami spoke to his group the morning of the tenth, he told them of the Emperor's decision and said that as the Emperor's decision was predicated on the assumption that the national polity would be preserved, it was too soon to say that the war had already ended. Lt. Col. Masao Inaba, of the Military Affairs Bureau, decided on his own that something must be sent out to the troops to keep up their morale, particularly the forces in Manchuria. Otherwise, he believed, unrest and disorder would follow. He evidently told this to the busy Anami and received overall approval of the idea.

Inaba went to work at once, drafting a statement to be broadcast to the troops overseas. He showed his first draft to

the Vice-Minister of War, General Tadaichi Wakamatsu,
the chief of the Military Affairs Bureau, General Yoshizumi,
and the chief of the Military Affairs Section, Colonel
Okisatsu Arao. They suggested various revisions and then
stamped the draft with their seals, to show their concurrence.
As General Anami could not be found, Colonel Arao, who
was to call at Anami's residence that night, was asked to get
the War Minister's approval.

After Colonel Arao had gone, Inaba had other visitors.
Two staff officers, one being Lt. Col. Masahiko Takeshita, an
intense , emotional man who was also General Anami's
brother-in-law, wanted Inaba's statement for the evening
news broadcast. As the revised draft had been taken to get
Anami's approval, Inaba and his friends had to search
through the wastebasket to find copies of the earlier draft.
Inaba made a clean copy, trying to get in the terms of the
revisions as he remembered them. The two staff officers went
away with the new document. It was presented to the radio
news people as a "must" statement from General Anami.

So, at a time when a statement from the Information
Bureau should have gone out, paving the way for the Japanese people to accept defeat, they heard the first supposed
words of their War Minister. The message said that there was
only one choice—to fight on to win the sacred war to preserve
the national polity. "We must fight on, even if we have to
chew grass and eat earth and live in the fields—for in our
death there is a chance of our country's survival. . . ." This
was followed by the somewhat ambiguous statement from
the Information Bureau.

If the Japanese people were confused by these remarks, and
later activities, it is understandable. Actually, to the Occi-
dental mind, even the statement from the Information
Bureau would not have been seen as a preparation for admission of defeat. But it is probable that the Japanese militarists
and the Information Bureau both placed too high a value on

the literal interpretation of the words. They may have taken their own pronouncements too seriously. People living in a nation where the news is tightly controlled soon learn to take what they read and hear with more than a grain of salt and to be able to read volumes between lines. The tendency is to search for what isn't being said. When the effects of the Hiroshima bomb were not being admitted, many Japanese realized there must have been a major disaster there by putting together the admission of a raid by a new type of bomb, as they kept calling it, and later items about temporary changes in railroad routings.

The Inaba–Anami statement certainly went contrary to the expressed wishes of the cabinet and at a different time might have caused a serious problem. As it was, Information Chief Shimomura, when trying to question Anami about the statement, got the impression that the War Minister was under extreme pressure from his younger officers. Supposedly, when Anami was questioned by others about the statement, he answered that of course the Army would keep on fighting until there was an actual surrender.

Now that the action for the final step had been taken, things should have quieted down, but key men in Tokyo and Washington said almost the same thing about the period: Secretary of State Byrnes wrote, "Never have I known time to pass so slowly," and Toshikazu Kase, the Foreign Office Secretary, described the days as "a lifetime of torture."

The period of waiting was much more active for some of the Japanese than it was for the Allies, who were waiting for answers and developments. Some of the Japanese were not waiting; they were anticipating, some one way, some another. Marquis Kido was busy seeing the Emperor and acting as liaison with various factions. From the remoteness of the Palace grounds, they worried about military and civil reaction to news of the loss of the war. Marquis Kido had figured the only way the country and the military could accept the

news would be if they heard it from the mouth of the
Emperor. He discussed this with the Emperor, who agreed
to do whatever was necessary.

What was lacking in Japan was a consensus. The Imperial
princes held a small conference of their own to hear Foreign
Minister Togo explain the situation to them. Afterwards,
those who had previously been inclined toward the fight-to-
the-death faction put up a solid front with the "reasonable
peace" side. Lurking in the minds of all, whether of ministerial rank or well below, was the specter of a hard-core
group of superpatriotic officers who would assassinate those
who didn't agree with them. This was no idle threat; it had
happened in the past and was in the process of happening
again.

While the Emperor and Kido were meeting with Suzuki
and Anami and Togo and others of the genro, fifteen officers
met in a bomb shelter at the War Office to determine the
proper steps to be taken so that the war would be continued.
They made a list of those who would have to go, including
Suzuki, Togo, and Kido. It might, they decided, even be
necessary to occupy the Imperial Palace in order to protect
the Emperor. The leader of the little group was Lieutenant
Colonel Takeshita, who thought he could count on the
support of his brother-in-law, General Anami.

As a matter of fact, Anami and a few others were key men
in the thinking of the plotters. If they could get some of the
big names, the rest would fall into line. They needed Anami,
General Tanaka of the Eastern Army, and General Mori,
the commander of the Imperial Guards, whose duty it was to
protect the Emperor. If General Mori opposed them, they
would have to get rid of him. The young officers who made
up the core of the rebels remained fixed, but the list of
people who worked with them changed from day to day and
from hour to hour. The young officers thought their activities
were based on the purest of patriotic motives. They con-

TOP: Admiral Mitsumasa Yonai (left), Prince Fumimaro Konoye
BOTTOM: Hideki Tojo (left), Emperor Hirohito, Koichi Kido
(*UPI photos*)

Crew for Nagasaki mission: Front row, left to right: Philip Barnes,
Jacob Beser, Fred Olivi, Kermit Beahan, Charles Albury, James Van
Pelt, Jr., Charles Sweeney, Frederick Ashworth. Back row, left to right:
John Kuharek, Abe Spitzer, Raymond Gallagher, Edward Buckley,
Albert Dehart.

(*UPI photos*)

Little Boy and Fat Man (full-scale models).

Ground zero shortly before and after the atomic bombing of Nagasaki.
(Ground zero is the spot directly below the detonation of the bomb.)
(ABOVE, *U.S. Air Force photo;* BELOW, *UPI photo*)

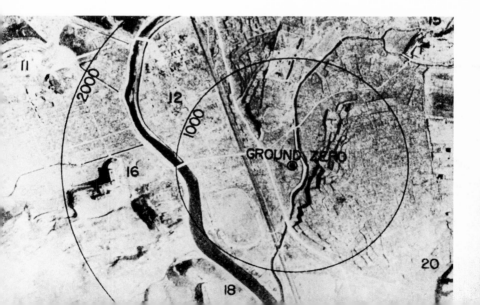

(UPI photos)

(facing p. 133)

Kantaro Suzuki (left) and Hirohito

Admiral Takijiro Onishi

General Shunroku Hata

Shigenori Togo

(UPI photos)

General Korechika Anami

Admiral Soemu Toyoda

General Yoshijiro Umezu

Kiichiro Hiranuma

(*UPI photos*)

vinced themselves that their attempt to change the present
course of the government would succeed, after which their
actions would be regarded as heroic rather than treasonous.
The honor of Japan would have been saved by these
patriotic, selfless men.

Their argument was helped by the wording of the Byrnes
note, which warned that the authority of the Emperor would
be subject to the Supreme Commander, that the ultimate
form of government would be established by the freely
expressed will of the Japanese people. To the reactionary
military men of Japan, this was the beginning of revolution!
What if the freely expressed will of the Japanese people
included getting rid of the Emperor? Putting the matter of
government up to the people was a ridiculous idea on the
face of it.

The Emperor had been informed by Marquis Kido of the
monitored news broadcast from America. Kido took up residence in the Palace, to be near the Emperor and out of the
range of possible assassins. He was right, of course; he was on
the first list of "traitors" to be disposed of. Foreign Minister
Togo, another "traitor," saw the use the military might try
to make of the Byrnes note, but believed the terms had to
be accepted. He thought it would preserve the Imperial
institutions and save the nation.

The younger officers, as some expected, decided the note
must be rejected. At eight in the morning, they stormed into
the headquarters of General Umezu and Admiral Toyoda,
demanding a public announcement of rejection of the terms.
They were so insistent and capable of causing so much
trouble that the Chiefs of Staff went to the Palace, despite
the early hour and lack of advance notification, and asked
for and received an audience.

It was not easy to determine whether the Army and Navy
staff heads were speaking for themselves out of conviction
or were being forced to say things (that they believed) by the

younger hotheads. At any rate, the Emperor expressed his
thanks for their opinion, but said that no action could be
taken until the official text was examined.

Admiral Yonai, the Navy Minister, was irked at his Chief
of Staff's unauthorized action and told him so in no uncertain
terms. General Anami, at heart more sympathetic to Umezu's
position, was a little more lenient when he heard about the
incident. But he was faced with another small crisis when a
dozen excited young officers rushed into his office. The
group's leader was again Colonel Takeshita, who stated flatly
that the proposed surrender should not take place and that
if it did, the War Minister should commit suicide. General
Anami just stared at his brother-in-law. There was no action,
just one-sided talk.

Foreign Minister Togo, who did not like the tone of portions of the note, had come to the conclusion that there was
nothing to do but accept its terms. The Emperor agreed with
his interpretation and asked Togo to pass it on to Suzuki.

But the aging Premier, who had put in a couple of days
and nights of activity that would have exhausted a much
younger and healthier man, was getting pressure from
another side. War Minister Anami and Baron Hiranuma
decided that they agreed; the Byrnes note should be rejected.
This seemed to be an about-face for Hiranuma, who had
been poking holes in the militarists' arguments. But he had
come to the conclusion that the latest note meant the end of
the power of the Emperor. Both Anami and Hiranuma had
decided that of those who had access to the Emperor, the one
they might be able to work on with the greatest chance of
success was Suzuki. Though a vacillator by nature, he had
stood firm during the last few hectic days. But he was an old
man, exhausted by the strain, and Hiranuma was able to persuade him that acceptance would mean the end of the
Imperial structure, which would mean a total change in

national polity. Anami reminded him that they had agreed to reject the note unless the national polity was guaranteed.

Anami then tried to get the aid of Prince Mikasa, the Emperor's youngest brother, known to some as the Red Prince. Prince Mikasa was regarded in some court circles as a socialist because he showed concern for the rights of the masses. He was, for a royal prince, a rebel and nonconformist. Anami hoped that he might be able to get Prince Mikasa to intercede with the Emperor and stop this surrender talk. Mikasa listened and said a flat no, pointing out that ever since the Manchurian incident, the Army had been acting contrary to the Emperor's desire.

The cabinet met in extraordinary session, resulting in more confusion. Foreign Minister Togo, who thought everything had been arranged, watched his "peace coalition" dissolve before his eyes as War Minister Anami played his few cards shrewdly. His arguments, helped by Baron Hiranuma, had turned Suzuki around, so that the premier was now speaking against acceptance of the peace terms.

Togo, amazed by this change in attitude, said that any further request by the Japanese at this point to change the conditions would lead to a breaking off of negotiations, which would be contrary to the expressed wishes of the Emperor. He described this behavior as senseless and angrily left the room.

Still wanting to blow off steam, he telephoned his aide, the Vice-Minister of Foreign Affairs, Shunichi Matsumoto, and told him what was taking place. Matsumoto, catching the crisis from the tone of his superior's voice, suggested that Togo play for time and have the meeting adjourned before there could be a vote.

The Foreign Minister returned to the meeting in time to hear Suzuki conclude a position statement—since Byrnes's note did not guarantee the rights of the Emperor, further clarification must be requested, and the nation should be prepared to continue the war. The Foreign Minister, controlling his anger and reverting to a more customary political smoothness, said the Premier's statements were worthy of careful consideration and suggested therefore that the meeting be adjourned to think about the situation and to await the arrival of the official communication, expected momentarily. He had taken the initiative away from Suzuki; the meeting broke up, with resumption of the discussion about acceptance of the Allied note to be the first order of business after the official cable was received.

Foreign Minister Togo had managed to control his anger for a time, but after the cabinet meeting was over, he sought out Premier Suzuki, telling the old man what he really thought about the change in attitude. He used similar tactics to those of Anami, for completely opposite purposes. Both men used the Emperor, Anami having appealed to Suzuki's regard for the untouchability of the Throne, Togo asking how Suzuki dared go contrary to the Emperor's expressed wish, threatening to ask the Emperor to request Suzuki's resignation. He then went to see Marquis Kido, asking his help in bringing Suzuki back to his earlier, more conciliatory position.

Vice-Minister Matsumoto, on getting a report of the occurrences at the cabinet meeting, came to the conclusion that the peace group needed time to repair their fences. To ensure this he spoke to the Duty Officer of the Telegraph Section of the Ministry, through whom the official text of the Allied reply would have to come, and instructed him that any official communication that came in during the night should be held up and dated the next morning.

Secretary Byrnes's official communication reached Tokyo at 6:40 P.M., Sunday, August 12. It was stamped in at 7:30 A.M., August 13.

Three hours after the official word was received, but ten hours before it was officially received, Premier Suzuki was called to the Palace office of Marquis Kido. Kido went over the grim war situation with him and ended with the more telling argument that this was the wish of the Emperor. Suzuki supposed that Kido was doing this at the Emperor's request and promised to stand by the decision to accept the Allied proposal.

War Minister Anami went home, and after spending some time with his family, received a visit from two of his men, Lt. Col. Masataka Ida, a traditional young officer in the Military Affairs Section, and Maj. Kenji Hatanaka, a pale, soft-featured officer, a particular pet of the War Minister's, and a fanatical war-to-the-bitter-ender. Their purpose was obvious; to work on Anami to prevent the acceptance of the Potsdam proclamation. General Anami listened without agreeing or disagreeing.

Several hours after midnight, Anami sent an aide with a verbal message to General Umezu. The aide was to get an opinion from the Chief of Staff about asking Field Marshal Hata to make an appeal to the Emperor, speaking for the senior officers, to refuse the Allied terms. Umezu surprisingly said no; he was in favor of accepting the terms.

During the night, aid for the peace faction came from an unexpected source—the Japanese government's Ministry in Sweden. Suemasa Okamoto, the Japanese minister in Stockholm, cabled the Foreign Office that the Byrnes note had not been received with complete approval by America's allies. The Soviet Union, in particular, and China had taken exception to the concept of retention of the Emperor. It was Okamoto's position that any further questions by Japan might well bring the negotiations to a complete halt and make the inevitable peace terms that much harsher.

General Anami started the day with a rather discouraging

interview with Marquis Kido at the Palace. Kido used every argument he could think of—if the objection was only about the status of the Emperor and the Emperor didn't object, why should they? Besides, the Emperor had made his decision and it had been communicated to the Allies. A change now would make him look like a fool; was that something Anami wanted?

These were all men of honor who were trying to work out a problem for their nation, their Emperor, and sometimes themselves. General Anami was regarded as a hard-liner, but his worst enemies among the peace faction would concede that he was not unreasonable, that he, personally, was quite willing to do whatever the Emperor wanted. But Anami represented the Army, and to a certain extent he was a prisoner of the fanatical young officers. He was stalling, trying to use his position inside the Army to keep these rebels in line. If he should resign, the government would fall, and under the conditions prevalent at the time, chaos would result.

General Umezu, considered a typical hard-liner, showed how difficult it was to classify people when he sent back word that he favored acceptance of the terms. Another of the Kwantung Army clique, he had been thought to prefer fighting on hopelessly to the dishonor of surrender. But his answer to Anami was a personal one; in meetings, he would back the Army line of no surrender. But when asked to help with a different move, on a personal basis, he wanted to do what he thought was best for the Emperor and his country.

The Navy Chief of Staff, Adm. Soemu Toyoda, the third hard-liner, was probably the most brilliant of the three and the most eloquent. The fact that he was in his present post was due to a mistake on the part of Admiral Yonai. When Yonai appointed Toyoda, he thought the beefy, pockmarked, sixty-year-old Navy man would be a part of the peace faction who would counter General Umezu, being a member of the same clan and coming from the same area. By the time Yonai discovered he was wrong about Toyoda, it was too late to remedy the situation. (This Adm. Soemu Toyoda is not to be confused with another, Adm. Teijiro Toyoda, who appeared in several previous cabinets.)

All these men were, in their own ways, dedicated and patriotic men who differed in the object of their dedication and what they considered was the "higher patriotism." And they changed. Baron Hiranuma, for instance, like Soemu Toyoda, had been an extreme xenophobe; but Hiranuma in his old age had mellowed, had turned against the Kwantung Army power group, had opposed war with America, had served a vital function in the meetings that brought about the first surrender notes and acceptance—and by August 12, had joined Anami in a last desperate effort to stall the surrender drive so that the person and institution of the Emperor could remain sacrosanct.

But by August 13, while the Japanese government seemed to be stalled at dead center, people and governments around the world were waiting for answers. Secretary of State Byrnes and President Truman were restive, unable to understand the reasons for delay, chafing at having to wait, wondering what more they could do to spur activity. In Moscow, according to some observers, the Russians were not disturbed by the delay; their armies were going through Manchuria at a great rate.

The Supreme War Council's meeting, which started at nine in the morning, was proceeding just as though there had been no crisis, no lecture from the Emperor, no decision. The council was still talking, still saying the same things, still split three to three. On this day, their deliberations were interrupted by a call for the two Chiefs of Staff, Umezu and Toyoda, from the Emperor. He pointed out that while diplomatic negotiations for a cease-fire were going on, military action should be kept to a minimum. They assured the Emperor that no aggressive moves would be made, that only such defensive action as was necessary would be taken, and returned to the deadlocked council meeting, which had recessed for lunch.

Nerves had been stretched to the breaking point by the combination of disaster and tension. It took a tremendous amount of control to stay cool, and not all the politicians and officers had that control at all times. Navy Minister Yonai, who had been forced to call down Admiral Toyoda for his unauthorized attempt to pressure the Emperor, now had a more personal confrontation with his Vice Chief of Staff. Adm. Takijiro Onishi, a headstrong but driving commander, was so upset about the course the government had been taking that he had been making allusions to Admiral Yonai's will to fight, or lack of it, that could only be considered a barely veiled charge of cowardice. Yonai asked stingingly how he dared talk in this fashion about his own minister, to which Onishi broke down and cried. He tried to apologize for his action, but could not get any words out. Admiral Yonai was a little surprised, but also relieved that Onishi was still capable of being reached by words.

Onishi had the reputation of being arrogant and difficult, as well as brilliant. He had helped draft the Yamamoto plan for the Pearl Harbor attack and had ordered the assault on Clark Field outside of Manila (after the Pearl Harbor attack) that practically eliminated American air power in the Far East for some time. He was not popular with many of his peers, being too aggressive, considered too showy, and condescending to those so insensitive to his superior abilities that they disagreed with him. He is given credit for having devised the Kamikaze attacks as a desperation measure in 1944. Being a colorful man, he also devised the costume the

Kamikaze pilots wore, the *hachimaki*, a white cloth worn around the forehead, theoretically to keep hair or sweat out of the eyes, but actually serving as a recognizable symbol of honor, being part of the costume worn by the Samurai many centuries earlier.

All through the islands, the young officers were upset at what they knew was happening and more upset by what they thought was happening but couldn't be sure of. Many civilians were in a similar state, wanting to show their patriotism and will to fight to the end, no matter what the politicians and "traitors around the Emperor" did. The Tokyo Metropolitan Police Department, aware of the possibilities of trouble, posted extra guards at various strategic points in the city. They also added to their surveillance of potential troublemakers certain military men who might be planning trouble.

The cabinet met again that afternoon, with no more sign of the necessary unanimity than before. Although Umezu and Toyoda were not cabinet members, Anami was not left as the lone holdout. A cabinet count showed twelve ministers favoring immediate acceptance and three opposed, with one undecided. In addition to Anami, the opposition included Genki Abe, the Home Minister, and Hiromasa Matsuzaka, the Minister of Justice.

Since Premier Suzuki could see no chance of obtaining the unanimous approval necessary, he adjourned the meeting, saying that once again he would have to ask the Emperor for a decision. General Anami, after adjournment, asked for two days before Suzuki again went to the Emperor, but Suzuki said no, he had to go at once.

This did not sound like the Suzuki of old, but he had his reasons. As he explained to someone who questioned him, if immediate action were not taken, the Russians would be in not only Manchuria but Korea and northern Japan as well. "If that happens, our country is finished. We must act now while our chief adversary is still the United States."

He knew that there were domestic reasons, as well, for immediate action. The announcement of another appeal to the Throne would spur the young officers to more action, which would probably be headstrong and might be fatal to the nation. As it was, the lid was barely being held down.

CHAPTER VII

"To Our Good and Loyal Subjects . . ."

At eight o'clock that night (August 13), a group of officers called on General Anami at his official residence. They wanted the approval of the War Minister for a coup d'état scheduled to take place at ten the next morning. The men, who thought highly of Anami, felt they needed his help for their venture to succeed.

Major Hatanaka spoke first, warning the War Minister that the peace advocates were planning his assassination if he continued to oppose an immediate surrender. General Anami laughed that off. He was well aware that some of the die-hard fanatics would plan to assassinate him if he changed his stand. He turned to Colonel Arao, head of the Military Affairs Section, who became the spokesman.

It was a peculiar position for the colonel. He was sure that Anami wouldn't support the rebels, but he was acting as their spokesman, explaining their plan to his superior. One part of the plan, on which he had insisted, was that the rebels had to obtain the consent of the four top military men—if not their help, at least word that they wouldn't oppose the plan. In addition to the most important one,

Anami, there were the Army Chief of Staff, Umezu; the Commander of the Eastern District Army, Gen. Seiichi Tanaka; and Gen. Takeshi Mori, Commander of the First Imperial Guards at the Palace. Other men in the rebels' plans were negative. Marquis Kido, Premier Suzuki, Foreign Minister Togo, and Admiral Yonai were to be imprisoned.

Japan could not surrender, the rebels said, until there was confirmation that there would be no change in her national polity. Although the decision had, admittedly, been made by the Emperor, it had to be determined to what extent he had been influenced by the men around him. That could come later, though. First, martial law had to be declared and the Palace isolated.

It was an ambitious scheme. It sounded crazy, but under the current conditions, it could succeed. General Anami, who had been walking a diplomatic tightrope for some time now, had to walk another one. He had to keep the coup from occurring yet still hold the confidence of the men who were pushing it. All he could do at the moment was play for time. He told the ten young officers he thought the plan had holes in it, that it was too general to be effective, that the details did not seem to have been worked out. He said that Colonel Arao should return in a couple of hours when he'd go over the plan with him. The men left, not satisfied but unable to complain. They hadn't received what they wanted—Anami's approval and consent—but he hadn't turned them down out of hand.

When Colonel Arao returned, General Anami said that he doubted very much that the plan could succeed. Arao eventually left, too, without a definite yes or no from the War Minister, which was the way Anami wanted it.

While Anami had been meeting with his rebellious officers, Foreign Minister Togo was having a hard time with the two Chiefs of Staff, General Umezu and Admiral Toyoda. They were trying to change his mind about the terms of the surrender; neither side was making progress. Their discussions were interrupted by the arrival of Admiral Onishi, the man who had been in tears before Admiral Yonai a little earlier. But Onishi now seemed to have recovered his old dash. He came to proffer an ambitious new scheme, although the word *ambitious* in this connection understates the idea. Onishi had come up with a last minute "certain victory" method. With the Emperor's approval, he was willing to sacrifice twenty million Japanese in Kamikaze attacks. It was a plan the ebullient admiral felt couldn't miss. It would, of course, permanently cripple the Japanese nation, possibly without any positive results, but Onishi couldn't see that. The Foreign Minister thanked him for his efforts, but said no.

The night ended without anything definite having taken place, and without the leaders of Japan getting much sleep. Except for the busy plotters, and the cabinet members and military leaders, the country seemed to be in a state of stunned suspense. Even the war, with the exception of the rapid Russian movements in Manchuria, had ground to a halt. The American naval and air forces were under orders to initiate no aggressive action. The Allies, who were waiting for a Japanese surrender, didn't want to make a move that might defer it. The Japanese were in such a state of confusion that any move they made would probably be the wrong one, certainly any military move would result in more trouble. For the people, there was pain and trouble enough to be found in the generally poor living conditions; the lack of food, shelter, and medicine; the loss of life, and even worse, the almost total loss of hope. These were conditions prevalent in the areas that had been hurt by conventional warfare; conditions in Hiroshima and Nagasaki were immeasurably worse.

The men in power in Japan knew they had no time to waste, and the need for an immediate action became more evident the next morning. Early in the morning of the fourteenth, Marquis Kido was shown a copy of a leaflet the Allies were dropping by the millions over the empire. It included the Japanese note of August 10 accepting the Potsdam terms, and Secretary Byrnes's answering note of the eleventh. When Kido saw the leaflet, he knew he had to do something at once. If enough of these fell into the hands of the troops, a military coup d'état would almost inevitably follow, and all their plans for an orderly surrender would be useless. A few minutes afterwards, he was closeted with the Emperor.

While Kido was talking to the Emperor, the young officers were again harassing Anami, trying to get an answer from him before the arrival of their ten o'clock deadline. They had asked General Mori and General Tanaka to come to the Ministry for a meeting. General Anami went with Colonel Arao to the office of the Chief of Staff, but General Umezu was still opposed to the idea of a coup.

After Marquis Kido had shown the leaflet to the Emperor, they agreed that another Imperial conference was necessary. Kido left to tell Suzuki, but found the aged Premier having his own troubles. He was trying to call the Supreme War Council together, but the Army wanted him to wait until one o'clock and the Navy, indefinitely. Before nine o'clock, Suzuki and Kido were back seeing the Emperor, who ordered the Imperial conference to be held at 10:30. Half an hour before the conference was to begin, the Emperor had called in what might be called Japan's elder statesmen, military branch, consisting of Field Marshal Hata, Field Marshal Sugiyama, and Fleet Admiral Nagano. He told them he was going to end the war and requested their support and the use of their influence with the Army and Navy.

At 10:30, the cabinet gathered in the same small, damp, hot room where the Supreme Council had met five days earlier. In many ways, this was a replay before a larger audience of the earlier meeting. The difference was that the urgencies were even greater now and that this time a decision would be legal. The Supreme Council, or Big Six, was extremely important, but to be legal under the constitution, the full cabinet had to agree to matters of such import.

As a result, the little room was even more crowded, and much hotter, as there were now twenty-four men in there, all suffering in their hastily donned uniforms. Actually an emergency meeting did not require formal dress. But this one had been called by the Emperor. Waiting for the Emperor was the full nineteen-man cabinet, the two Chiefs of Staff, and such dignitaries as Baron Hiranuma.

In an unplanned way, the sudden meeting thwarted the military plotters. Colonel Takeshita and Major Hatanaka had received the impression that General Umezu had withdrawn his objections and would now join them. They dashed over to tell General Anami, convinced that they were now on their way to protect the Emperor—their way—only to discover that Anami had left for a meeting at the Palace. When they got there, he had already entered and could not be reached.

For the earlier meeting, there had been two facing rows of chairs, behind two narrow tables. The decor had been changed slightly to fit the situation. There were now two rows of chairs along each wall, with a larger table, covered with gold brocade cloth, between them. At the end of the table, by the entrance door, was a single straight armchair. At 10:50, clad in a plain military uniform, the Emperor entered and sat at the chair at the head of the table.

Later, Cabinet Secretary Sakomizu said that he had been worrying about the ability of the Premier to conduct the meeting. Suzuki had appeared particularly vague that morning and had not even prepared a speech, nor had there been time to get one ready for him. But the old man rose to the challenge. He explained, briefly and clearly, that the meeting had been called by His Majesty so that discussion about acceptance of the Allied note could take place in his presence. Suzuki then outlined the divergent points of view that had kept the council and cabinet from unanimous decisions during the past few days and called on the dissenters to explain themselves. Anami and Umezu both spoke briefly and without much ardor. Admiral Toyoda then rose and made a much longer speech, well-reasoned, deeply felt, and superficially convincing. But he had nothing new to say, nothing that those present had not heard before.

When the speakers had finished, Suzuki arose, apologized to His Majesty for presenting him with division instead of unanimity, and asked again for an Imperial decision.

The Emperor stood up to speak. Suffering under the handicap of having to say things he didn't want to say, he had a great deal of difficulty. It was a very emotional time for the Emperor and for his listeners. Repeatedly, during the short speech, the Emperor had to stop to recover his aplomb, as well as his voice. According to people present, he said:*

HIROHITO'S SPEECH TO CABINET, A.M. AUGUST 14, 1945

I have listened carefully to all of the arguments opposing Japan's acceptance of the Allied reply as it stands. My own opinion, however, has not changed. I shall now restate it. I have examined the conditions prevailing in Japan and in the rest of the world, and I believe that a continuation of the war offers nothing but continued destruction. I have studied the terms of the Allied reply, and I have come to the conclusion that they represent a virtually complete acknowledgment of our position as we outlined it in the note dispatched a few days ago. In short, I consider the reply to be acceptable.

---

* No transcript of the speech was made. This is an accepted version according to the memories and records of men who were there, including Hiroshi Shimomura, Director of the Cabinet's Information Bureau; Hisatsune Sakomizu, the Chief Cabinet Secretary; Baron Hiranuma; Marquis Kido; and others.

Although some of you are apprehensive about the preservation of the national structure, I believe that the Allied reply is evidence of the good intentions of the enemy. The conviction and resolution of the Japanese people are, therefore, the most important consideration. That is why I favor acceptance of the reply.

I fully understand how difficult it will be for the officers and men of the Army and the Navy to submit to being disarmed and to see their country occupied. I am aware also of the willingness of the people to sacrifice themselves for their nation and their Emperor. But I am not concerned with what may happen to me. I want to preserve the lives of my people. I do not want them subjected to further destruction. It is indeed hard for me to see my loyal soldiers disarmed and my faithful ministers punished as war criminals.

If we continue the war, Japan will be altogether destroyed. Although some of you are of the opinion that we cannot completely trust the Allies, I believe that an immediate and peaceful end to the war is preferable to seeing Japan annihilated. As things stand now, the nation still has a chance to recover.

I am reminded of the anguish Emperor Meiji felt at the time of the Triple Intervention. Like him, I must bear the unbearable now and hope for the rehabilitation of the country in the future. But this is indeed a complex and difficult problem that cannot be immediately solved. However, I believe it can be done if the people will join together in a common effort. I will do everything I can to help.

I cannot express the sorrow I feel as I think of all who were killed on the battlefield or in the homeland and of their bereaved families. I am filled with anxiety about the future of those who have been injured or who have lost all their property or their means of livelihood. I repeat, I will do everything in my power to help.

As the people of Japan are unaware of the present situation, I know they will be deeply shocked when they hear of our decision. If it is thought appropriate that I explain the matter to them personally, I am perfectly willing to go before the microphone. The troops, particularly, will be dismayed at our decision. The War Minister and the Navy Minister may not find it easy to persuade them to accept the decision. I am willing to go wherever necessary to explain our action.

I desire the Cabinet to prepare as soon as possible an Imperial Rescript announcing the termination of the war.

The Emperor rose, turned, and left the room. A few minutes afterwards, having recovered their composure, his ministers and aides left too. Once again, the Emperor had spoken, resolving all questions.

And once again, nothing was actually settled.

The cabinet then had to prepare and approve the rescript for the Emperor's signature. Chief Cabinet Secretary Sakomizu, asking for an assistant, Michio Kihara, a former newspaperman, went to his office at Suzuki's residence. The two men, expecting this turn of events, had been working on drafts of rescripts. Now they had to rewrite them to fit the Emperor's words. Sakomizu came to the conclusion that two rescripts would be necessary, one announcing the end of the war to the people and another meant for the troops.

The cabinet members were not in the mood for lunch; they decided they would meet again at one P.M. Waiting for War Minister Anami was his brother-in-law, Colonel Takeshita; they met for their promised private talk. Takeshita asked Anami to use his authority to mobilize the troops to maintain security, adding that there was much Anami could do at the cabinet meeting. Anami said no, that the Emperor had made his decision and that as a Japanese soldier, he must obey. Takeshita then asked the general to resign, thus bringing down the cabinet and sparing the Army and Japan this humiliation, at least for the moment. Anami refused, saying the war would end anyway. Takeshita suddenly realized that further conversation was useless; Anami was not going to budge from his position.

Anami made his way to the War Ministry and was about to sit at his desk when a group of young officers broke in, having heard stories that the Emperor had opted for peace at any price. Their curiosity and excitement were almost visible as they asked what had happened and what the War Minister intended to do, so sure were they that he would never give the order to surrender. Anami told them what had happened, adding, "We have no choice but to abide by his decision. It is based on his confidence in our loyalty."

The officers seemed confused. Just a few days before, a proclamation issued under his name had advocated continuing the war; now he was talking peace. Colonel Ida, a spokesman for the bitter-enders, got up enough courage to ask why he had changed his mind. Anami, who knew how the young officers felt and could sympathize with them, said that the Emperor had personally asked him to, no matter how difficult, and in that case he could no longer oppose his view to the Emperor's decision. Repeating what he had told some of the men five days earlier, Anami said, "The Emperor has given his decision, and we have no choice whatsoever but to obey it. Anyone who disagrees will have to do so over my dead body."

Once again the young officers left the War Minister quietly, most of them seeming abashed.

The cabinet gathered at one o'clock, as expected, to approve the Emperor's decision. Then they had to agree on the wording of the Imperial rescript ending the war. Suzuki opened the meeting by expressing his anger at the fact that twice they had had to trouble the Emperor to decide between two opposing factions. "It should not have happened," said Suzuki. "It was an affront to the Throne. It happened only because we did not try hard enough." Anami sat back in his chair, relaxed. He had done all that any one man could do.

The state that Japan was in showed the futility of trying to continue the war. It was bad enough to be trying to fight a war when there were desperate shortages of almost all war materials, of everything in fact, except manpower. It was almost impossible to move materials by train or truck, and becoming impossible to do so by water, an important factor in the Japanese economy. The ubiquitous B-29s, in addition to being used as bombers, were being used as mine layers, particularly in the Inland Sea. The Allied air raids had cut Japanese communications to small pieces. This had its inevitable effect on manufacturing, which was already troubled enough by material shortages and then by having key plants bombed. On top of all the other troubles, there was the horrifying, growing, food shortage. The rice crop was small; the lack of communications made help from other areas and abroad almost impossible.

It was no wonder the Emperor did not want his people subjected to further destruction. But he, and his top advisers, knew his people well enough to know how shocking news of the true situation was going to be. For this reason, the announcement had to come from the Emperor himself.

Except for the cabinet, and a few key advisers, the first Japanese to know that the Emperor himself would talk to the people were three top men of NHK, the Japanese Broadcasting Corporation. While the cabinet was reassembling to go over the wording of the Imperial rescript, they were asked to appear at the Information Bureau. There the radio men were told by a cabinet secretary that an Imperial rescript ending the war would soon be released, to be read by the Emperor. The question now being considered was whether it would be done live by the Emperor, or recorded. As soon as that was decided, they would be notified. In the meanwhile, they were to make preparations for the event, either way.

The Japanese electronics industry was a postwar phenomenon. Radio recordings in Japan at the time were just that —put on records. The tape recorder was a thing of the future as was, for Japan, the wire recorder. Radios had not yet been miniaturized and transistorized. Radio news, through Domei and NHK, was a government monopoly. The three NHK directors were stunned at the news that the Emperor would speak. He had never before spoken on the radio to the Japanese people, although a few, by mistake, had once heard his voice.

That error had taken place seventeen years earlier, less than a month after Hirohito had ascended to the throne, at a broadcast of a military review honoring the event. Although the microphone had been placed fifty yards behind the royal enclosure, some peculiarity of acoustics caused it to pick up the Emperor's voice and broadcast it. This created quite a furor at the time, but the incident eventually died down. Most people who knew about the event had forgotten it.

But this was a different matter—the Emperor was going to speak directly to the people, the hundred million of Japan, few of whom had ever seen him (and then at a distance) and none who expected ever to hear him. The Emperor of Japan was not a politician; he did not have to go before the people for votes. He was not, in one way, a member of the government, and yet in another way, he was the government. It was a peculiar position in which to be, an anomaly for the twentieth century. Practically everything in Japan was done in his name, including many things of which he would have disapproved. He was revered as the living descendant of Amaterasu, the Goddess of the Sun. As an educated man, however, trained in science, it is reported that he did not believe in the myth of his family's origin. As the head of the family, on the other hand, he made no public statement that he did not believe he was directly descended from the sun until well after the war was over.

The point is that while in most other nations, radio was used regularly by government and royalty, as well as by religious leaders, in Japan the fact that the Emperor would speak to his people in this direct fashion was going to impress and amaze his subjects. That he had already injected himself into military affairs by speaking his mind, first to the Big Six and then to the cabinet, was known only to the people who had heard him and a few other officials. The NHK directors were told that the cabinet had decided it would be presumptuous to ask the Emperor to speak directly to the people; instead, he ought to be asked to record it. A recording team was consequently requested to be at the Imperial Household Ministry on the Palace grounds at three that afternoon.

Selecting the equipment they would need—two recorders, two sets of recording amplifiers, a microphone, all of the best then available in Japan—the team set it up in the second floor room selected for the purpose. When asked to arrange, if possible, for the Emperor to hear an immediate playback, they left for the downtown building, where a secret underground broadcasting station had been set up in case the NHK building should be destroyed, dismantled the playback machine, and brought it to the palace.

The Emperor had also made an offer to speak to the Army and Navy officers if it should be necessary. Both General Anami and Admiral Yonai refused the offer, saying they would speak to, and guarantee, the obedience of their men. Rumors were flying all over the capital that a revolt, a coup d'état, was being planned. This was a domestic reason for making haste with the Emperor's broadcast; the other reason, of course, was so that the Allies would know, officially, that the war was over, and would not take any further action. It would be a public acknowledgment of the private diplomatic cables. Unofficially, the Allies heard the news that afternoon. An English-language Domei overseas transmission said: "It is learned that an Imperial message accepting the Potsdam proclamation is forthcoming soon."

That was 2:49 P.M., August 14. The message was correct in thought, but twenty-one hours and eleven minutes early.

Wheels were turning, but they were often inside other wheels and often at cross purposes. Japan's struggle against surrender was continuing despite the efforts of the Emperor, of such people as Togo and Kido and Suzuki and Yonai, and even after a man like Anami had given in, in principle.

While the men from the broadcasting studios waited, the cabinet continued its deliberations. Now it was a matter of wording and legality. There was a question of whether the Imperial rescript had to be approved by the Privy Council, since legally the acceptance of the Potsdam proclamation was similar to the conclusion of a treaty. The Director of the Legislative Bureau was asked to study the question while the cabinet recessed. He returned with his opinion—the approval of the Privy Council was not necessary—and the cabinet resumed its deliberations, with constant interruptions as ministers were called out to answer requests from their departments. The men from NHK talked and waited.

While the cabinet was meeting, Marquis Kido, the Lord Privy Seal, went to see Prince Konoye at the prince's request. Konoye was not always popular, nor had he been effective; he was, however, a consistent advocate of peace. He had been disturbed by a report that something was stirring in the Imperial Guards Division. Throughout his life, Konoye had feared a communist or socialist uprising; now he was worried about the military. Lt. Gen. Takeshi Mori, head of the First Imperial Guards Division at the Palace, was regarded as being totally loyal to the Emperor. It was his job to guard the Imperial family and grounds, and no one doubted that he would do so. A solid, sad-faced officer, there was no nonsense about him, nor would he permit any.

While the informed worried about the delay and the uninformed worried about conditions, the cabinet went right on deliberating at what seemed to be a snail's pace. What was detaining them now was the persistent and stubborn General Anami. They had all been a little afraid of the

War Minister, afraid he might still do something to throw a monkey wrench into the machinery. He had been too calm, too agreeable, behaving as though he had something up his sleeve, such as his written-out resignation.

But now he wasn't being so agreeable; he was being stubborn, defending his beloved Army. He was against using the sentence: "The war situation grows more unfavorable to us every day." These words made, he argued, all the recent announcements of military achievement appear to be lies, which many were. Anami wanted the sentence changed to: "The war situation has not turned in our favor." The argument raged, as previous arguments had, with Admiral Yonai being particularly outspoken and angry. The rest of the cabinet tried to convince Anami otherwise, but he would not be budged.

General Anami wasn't giving the real reason, however, for his objections. He knew the war was lost, he knew the war situation had grown more unfavorable every day, but he was trying to make the announcement of defeat more palatable to his troops. Whether use of this euphemism was to protect his Army from scorn or whether it was to head off a possible revolt or attempt at a coup by some of the Army will never be known. It could have been a little of both. Whatever the motive, cabinet action was stalled on the wording of the rescript, just as it had been stalled twice on acceptance of terms. And time was growing shorter.

Admiral Yonai was called away to the Navy Ministry for a short time. Before he left, he told the Cabinet Secretary, Sakomizu, to hold out for the original wording. But when the admiral came back, he spoke a few words to General Anami, and then surprisingly said, "I would like to see the phrasing of the Imperial rescript revised in accordance with the War Minister's desires."

The cabinet breathed a collective sigh of relief. Although this was most unlike Yonai, everyone was pleased to have cleared this hurdle. They wondered, of course, why the admiral had suddenly changed his mind. Nothing that was said to him during his brief visit to the Navy Ministry would have had that effect. He must have realized, while out of the room, that Anami wasn't being obstinate, but doing what he felt he must.

There was one more problem of phraseology to solve before the cabinet was through with its work. The rescript, as amended, was sent to the Palace for approval and for final copying. The mimeographed sheets were handed to two officials so that they could copy them with brushes on thick paper. There were so many changes, so many words and phrases scratched out and new ones inserted, that it was not easy to read, much less to copy. But two accurate copies had to be made, and quickly, so that the job of accepting peace terms could be completed. Because this was a royal rescript, the work had to be done by hand in the traditional fashion, and with the traditional flourishes.

While the two copyists were busy at their work, the cabinet was considering the best time for release of the Emperor's speech. Togo and Yonai suggested the next morning at seven. General Anami wanted to delay it by a day, so as to have time to issue orders to the troops to lay down their arms and to make sure the orders were received and obeyed. Others, although they could see the point of waiting, felt that the Allies, as well as the people of Japan, had to be informed as soon as possible. The Director of the Information Bureau, Hiroshi Shimomura, pointing out that too many people would be out of reach of their radios for an early morning broadcast to be effective, and that too long a delay might be dangerous, suggested noon, and the cabinet agreed.

At the Palace, Gen. Shigeru Hasunuma, the Emperor's chief aide-de-camp, was waiting like everyone else. While talking with another aide, Colonel Seiki, two young officers entered, saying they'd heard the Emperor would be making a broadcast and asking what time it would be made. They explained that they were staff officers of the Imperial Guards Division and had to prepare the division for use, in the event action should prove necessary. The Emperor's aides offered no information. The visitors then asked whether the recording had been made; the aides answered that as far as they knew, it had not been and that they didn't know when it would be. The two staff officers started to press for more information, thought better of it, and left. Colonel Seiki was puzzled; he thought he had seen them before, but he didn't know their names. Another officer, who had seen the incident, said that one of the men was probably Major Koga, a staff officer of the Imperial Guards, and the son-in-law of Gen. Hideki Tojo, the hidebound militarist, former Kwantung Army Chief of Staff, who had been Premier at the time of Pearl Harbor.

The acceptable copies of the Imperial rescript were completed and one given to Marquis Kido to take to the Emperor. He wanted five minor changes made. The cabinet was told about these, and the copiers made the changes. Under normal circumstances these two rescripts would have been done over, completely. But the most important thing now was time. Even for the Japanese, traditionalists who often put style and form above content, the important thing now was to make public these rescripts. Because of the changes that had been made and the need for speed, Premier Suzuki found himself handing the Emperor a document that was, in the Gilbert and Sullivan tradition, "a thing of shreds and patches." The Emperor signed "Hirohito" at the bottom of the rescript, the Imperial seal was affixed, and the date, August 14, 1945 ("14th day, 8th month, 20th year of Showa") was recorded. As far as the Japanese Emperor was concerned, this brought the ordeal of the fighting war to an end. The ordeal that was to be the first small step to peace was just beginning.

The nine o'clock news that night announced that an important broadcast would be made at noon the next day which everyone in Japan was expected to listen to. The same information was given to the Tokyo newspapers, though too late for the first edition of the daily papers. Now that the Emperor had signed the rescript, the Foreign Office could cable its ambassadors in Switzerland and Sweden to transmit a message to the governments of the United States and China, of Britain and the Soviet Union.

Referring to Byrnes's note of August 11, the message said that His Majesty had issued an Imperial rescript accepting the Potsdam Declaration. It added that he was prepared to ensure the signature of the necessary terms for carrying out the provisions of the Potsdam Declaration, as well as to issue commands to the armed forces to cease operations and to surrender.

A little before ten, Premier Suzuki affixed his signature to the rescript, and one by one the other ministers followed. Some time around 11 P.M., the Emperor left the Gobunko, where he was then living, for the Household Ministry, where he was to record his message. As he was preparing to make his debut, the cabinet members were beginning to recover from their ordeal.

General Anami approached Foreign Minister Togo, bowed, and said, "I have seen the text of the note the Foreign Office is sending to accompany our acceptance of the Potsdam proclamation, and I would like to thank you for it." Togo smiled; he had done simply what he had said he would do—ask the enemy for certain concessions Anami had wanted as part of the conditions of acceptance. Part of the note had said:

Disarming of the Japanese forces being a most delicate task, as it involves over three million officers and men overseas and having direct bearing on their honor, the Japanese Government will, of course, take utmost pains. But it is suggested that the best and most effective method would be that under the command of His Majesty the Emperor, the Japanese forces are allowed to disarm themselves and surrender arms of their own accord.

Anami expressed his gratitude and said, "I feel I owe you an apology for some of the things I may have said in the heat of argument."

Togo returned the bow, and the two men, former enemies, smiled and parted.

Anami then went to the next-door office of the Premier, who was sitting behind his desk talking with Chief Cabinet Secretary Sakomizu and a few others. Suzuki rose as Anami stood by his desk. The discussion was similar to the one he had had with Togo, but longer. Anami said that he had expressed opinions he held as a representative of the Army, possibly too strongly at times, but that his intention was to assist the Premier, at which he had not always been successful, for which he apologized.

Suzuki came around the desk, put his hand on the general's shoulder, and thanked him for his frankness, saying he knew the man had always been motivated primarily by patriotism. The two men spoke for a few minutes more, with Suzuki saying he felt the Emperor was now safe as was Japan. Anami agreed. "I believe that if the Emperor and the people are together, Japan will recover."

Anami brought out a small, newspaper-wrapped package and gave it to Suzuki, explaining that it contained cigars. Since he didn't smoke, he thought the Prime Minister should use them. He saluted and left, with Sakomizu seeing him to the door.

The room was silent until Suzuki spoke. "I think the War Minister came to say good-bye."

And at another part of the Palace grounds, Director

Shimomura of the Information Bureau was escorting the Emperor into the brightly lighted room where he would make his recording. There were only a few men present for the historic occasion; in addition to the Emperor and Shimomura, there were two chamberlains, Mitsui and Toda, with the Emperor; the Imperial Household Minister; and the Grand Chamberlain. In the next room, its doors open, were men from the Information Bureau, the Japan Broadcasting Corporation, and the Imperial Household Ministry.

As the Emperor approached the microphone in the middle of the room, he asked how loud he should speak. Answering that the Emperor should use his ordinary tones, Shimomura raised one hand in a signal to begin the recording. The Emperor spoke with a great deal more confidence than he had shown before the council or the cabinet. It was much easier now, the decision had been made. He looked at the paper in his hand and began reading:

TO OUR GOOD AND LOYAL SUBJECTS:

After pondering deeply the general trends of the world and the actual conditions obtaining in Our Empire today, We have decided to effect a settlement of the present situation by resorting to an extraordinary measure.

We have ordered Our Government to communicate to the Governments of the United States, Great Britain, China and the Soviet Union that Our Empire accepts the provisions of their Joint Declaration.

To strive for the common prosperity and happiness of all nations as well as the security and well-being of Our subjects is the solemn obligation which has been handed down by Our Imperial Ancestors and which lies close to Our heart.

Indeed, We declared war on America and Britain out of Our sincere desire to ensure Japan's self-preservation and the stabilization of East Asia, it being far from Our Thought either to infringe upon the sovereignty of other nations or to embark upon territorial aggrandizement.

But now the war has lasted for nearly four years. Despite the

best that has been done by everyone—the gallant fighting of the
military and naval forces, the diligence and assiduity of Our
servants of the State, and the devoted service of Our one hundred
million people—the war situation has developed not necessarily
to Japan's advantage, while the general trends of the world have
all turned against her interest.

Moreover, the enemy has begun to employ a new and most
cruel bomb, the power of which to do damage is, indeed, incal-
culable, taking the toll of many innocent lives. Should We continue to fight, not only would it result in an ultimate collapse
and the obliteration of the Japanese nation, but also it would
lead to total extinction of human civilization.

Such being the case, how are We to save the millions of Our
subjects, or to atone Ourselves before the hallowed spirits of Our
Imperial Ancestors? This is the reason why We have ordered the
acceptance of the provisions of the Joint Declaration of the
Powers.

We cannot but express the deepest sense of regret to Our Allied
nations of East Asia, who have consistently cooperated with the
Empire towards the emancipation of East Asia.

The thought of those officers and men as well as others who
have fallen in the fields of battle, those who died at their posts
of duty, or those who met with untimely death and all their
bereaved families, pains Our heart night and day.

The welfare of the wounded and the war-sufferers, and of those
who have lost their homes and livelihood, are the objects of Our
profound solicitude.

The hardships and sufferings to which Our nation is to be
subjected hereafter will certainly be great. We are keenly aware
of the inmost feelings of all of you, Our subjects. However, it is
according to the dictates of time and fate that We have resolved
to pave the way for a grand peace for all the generations to come
by enduring the unendurable and suffering what is unsufferable.

Having been able to safeguard and maintain the structure of
the Imperial State, We are always with you, Our good and loyal
subjects, relying upon your sincerity and integrity.

Beware most strictly of any outbursts of emotion which may
engender needless complications, or any fraternal contention and

strife which may create confusion, lead you astray and cause you to lose the confidence of the world.

Let the entire nation continue as one family from generation to generation, ever firm in its faith in the imperishability of its sacred land, and mindful of its heavy burden of responsibility and of the long road before it.

Unite your total strength, to be devoted to construction for the future. Cultivate the ways of rectitude, foster nobility of spirit, and work with resolution—so that you may enhance the innate glory of the Imperial State and keep pace with the progress of the world.

"Was it all right?" The Emperor asked the question as soon as he had finished, like any mere mortal making his first recording, or his hundredth. The chief engineer said that although there were no technical errors, a few words were not entirely clear. The Emperor told Shimomura that he would like to make another recording, as he was aware that his voice had been pitched too low.

Once again, the Emperor spoke into the microphone while engineers fiddled with their dials and the turntable turned. This time, his voice was too high and he seemed more tense —he even missed a word. When he finished, he felt that the second recording wasn't right either, and said he would be willing to make a third one. After a certain amount of pala-ver, it was decided that a third recording would not be necessary. Coming at the end of a long and tiring day, it had been quite a task for the frail Emperor. It was brutally hot in the studio, to add to the troubles. After the Emperor left, it was decided to use the first recording.

The records were put into metal cases, the lids of which didn't fit very well. Motohike Kakei, Chief of the Ministry's General Affairs Section, came up with two cotton bags, khaki-colored, used to hold air-defense uniforms. Once the cases were put in the bags, came the question of where to store the recording until it was to be used. The Imperial Household Ministry thought that the Japan Broadcasting Corporation should handle the matter, but these people felt it would be disrespectful to the Emperor to bring the records to the station in the middle of the night. Besides, they said, in view of the rumors floating around about a military take-over, the records would probably be safer in the Imperial Household Ministry. That couldn't be disputed at the time.

But Motohike Kakei had no idea where to keep the records, now that he had them. He asked the two Imperial chamberlains who were present to take charge of them. Yoshihiro Tokugawa agreed and took the two small bags from Kakei. Although there were specific places designated for keeping objects belonging to or relating to the Emperor, no one before Chamberlain Tokugawa had had the problem of finding a safe place for a prerecorded Imperial radio talk. Mr. Tokugawa decided to put the speech into a small safe in a small office, used by one of the Emperor's retinue. He then locked the safe and put piles of paper in front of it to hide it from sight.

Those amateurish moves were to become quite important.

After Shimomura of the Information Bureau had seen the records handed over to Chamberlain Tokugawa, he phoned the Premier's official residence to report to him, but was told that Suzuki was on his way home. Consequently, Shimomura spoke to Cabinet Secretary Sakomizu instead, reporting that the Emperor had made the recording and that there had been no trouble. "We're in the clear," he said.

"Let's hope so," Sakomizu answered, "but the night isn't over yet."

CHAPTER VIII

The Plot and the Plotters

For some of the rebellious young officers, it was to be a night of intensive effort, a night of alternating ups and downs, a night of high and dashed hopes, of high and low cunning, of achievement and futility.

It had started, for some, much earlier; started, really, when they heard rumors that the military was going to surrender. To some of these men, this was the last word in the unthinkable, as ridiculous, in a different way, as for the British to imagine Her Majesty doing a music hall turn. The Japanese Army had no tradition of surrender; there was no word for it in their code of conduct. The men, led by their officers, were expected to die for their Emperor and country, if not by enemy action, then by killing themselves. The battle for Okinawa, the last big land fight of the war, was an exception. In a hopeless effort, the Japanese Army suffered over one hundred thousand casualties, but what amazed some military experts was that Allied forces took more than seven thousand prisoners, by far the largest haul of Japanese military personnel taken during the war in the Pacific.

The young officers who led the revolt against surrender

differed widely in their backgrounds and education. The things they had in common were their military training, the fact that some of them had known no other life except the military, and their stubborn loyalty to what they considered their duty: to protect their Emperor, whether or not he wished to be protected. Like many zealots, they were convinced that they were right and would be vindicated by history.

Some of them came from Japan's best families, some probably had Samurai ancestry, some were well educated in Japanese and Western schools, some were the sons of poor workers and peasants and had reached officer status by demonstrating exceptional ability or bravery in the field. But whether commanding troops or holding down a desk job, they seemed to have the same outlook on their duties and what they should do about the approaching shameful end of the war.

One of the young officers, on August 13, had managed to send out a message from Imperial Headquarters saying that the Imperial forces had received new orders and had accordingly resumed operations against the enemy. This message had gone out to all the newspapers and the Japanese Broadcasting Corporation while the cabinet was meeting and debating over the meaning of certain phrases in Secretary Byrnes's note. Fortunately, the editor of one of the papers, knowing the purpose of the cabinet meeting, thought there was something fishy about this announcement. He did a little checking by telephone, discovered that no one in authority knew anything about it, and had the item killed, not only for his paper but for all news media. If it had gone out, Allied forces, poised for action but held back, might have been unchained, another atomic bomb or two might have been prepared . . . and who would have believed the Japanese government when it said the whole thing had been a mistake?

How could a government make an official mistake with an announcement from Imperial Headquarters?

Most of the antisurrender activity seemed to be centered, quite naturally, in Tokyo. In the War Ministry, there was a group that was made up of fanatics from several sections and spent much of its time and energy trying to round up sympathizers. If they had been able to get together with some of the more individualistic rebels at other headquarters and bases, they might have been able to stall or stop the peace negotiations, install a military government, and continue the war until they and their entire nation were crushed beyond any chance of short-term revival.

One of the rebellious officers who didn't connect with the Tokyo group was a Naval Captain, Yasuna Kozono. An old die-hard rather than a young firebrand, he did not plan to act without giving warning. When he heard about the possibility of surrender, he fired off long telegrams of protest to the Navy Minister and other top officials. Captain Kozono was the commander of the 302d Air Corps at the largest air base in Japan—Atsugi. At this stage of the war, the 302d was in a peculiar state of readiness. It had a number of new planes and was kept on a continuous twenty-four-hour alert. Ringed by batteries of antiaircraft guns, the Atsugi base had underground quarters for flight crews, other underground facilities for aircraft repairs and the like, and stores of food and ammunition to last for two years.

Captain Kozono, determined to use these resources, had told his deputies about his plans, which included an August fifteenth dawn attack, using all available aircraft, on all enemy troop positions they could reach. Captain Kozono had decided that he would fight on alone, if necessary, no matter what the Army did, and that he would take command of the Navy and lead it in a continuation of the war; to do so was the highest form of patriotism, indeed acceptance of orders to disarm and cease fire would be tantamount to high treason.

Captain Kozono was activated by what were, to him, the highest of motives. He also had malaria. At a time when his men expected to hear from him at any moment to give the signal for the attack, he was in his room, immobilized by the characteristic chills and fever of malaria.

Another group was equally determined to uphold the honor of Japan in the traditional fashion. This group was made up of some young people from Yokohama, the big industrial and port city only a few miles south-southwest of Tokyo, on Tokyo Bay. The Yokohamans were led by Captain Takeo Sasaki, a bearded young Army officer who had decided he would continue to prosecute the war despite the machinations of the cowardly statesmen. Having come to this conclusion, on the night of August 14, he went to the headquarters of the Yokohama Guards to issue an emergency order to them to kill the Premier. To his amazement, his four company commanders flatly refused. They told him they would not move without orders from General Harada.

Like many men who are convinced of the righteousness of their cause, Captain Sasaki had not been quiet about his plans. As a result, General Harada had issued specific instructions to the company commanders that if Sasaki came up with any such orders, they were to be ignored. Sasaki did not know this, but he knew he had no followers. All he could do was warn the company commanders not to try to stop him and storm off into the night.

In the gray, predawn hours, Captain Sasaki and thirty-six men were driving toward Tokyo on Route Two, the highway from Yokohama. Most of Captain Sasaki's group were Imperial Army men he didn't know, but who had shown a willingness to follow him. Five of his followers were students and two were members of the Yokohama Youth Corps. They had two light machine guns, as well as swords and pistols, and they were going to start their patriotic work by assassinating the Premier, a fate the old naval hero had long feared.

Sasaki and his group pulled up in front of the Premier's official residence just as light was beginning to break. They set up the two machine guns facing the front entrance, and Captain Sasaki gave the order to fire. Cabinet Secretary Sakomizu, awakened by the noise, thought enemy troops were attacking the city, but his younger brother had looked out and seen that the force was Japanese. The two Sakomizus left through an emergency exit, glad that Suzuki had decided to spend what was left of the night at his private residence.

Sasaki, figuring he had silenced all opposition, went to the front gate and ordered it opened. A guard at the gate told the captain that he, too, felt that all the traitors should be liquidated and that Suzuki was at his home in Maruyama. Sasaki had some oil poured on the carpet by the front door, but it was too heavy and refused to light as planned. Finally they were able to set it afire, got back into the truck and car that had brought them, and went off in search of Suzuki. The fire, which did not burn well, was easily put out by some guards and others left in the house.

At about the same time, seven men of a different group attacked the residence of Marquis Kido; they were driven off by the guards after a fierce but brief battle.

The phone rang at the Suzuki residence at Maruyama. Hajime Suzuki, the Premier's son and chief aide, answered. He was told that soldiers had tried to burn down the official residence and were now on the way to Maruyama. Hajime got his mother and father up and into his car, parked on a narrow lane in front of the house, and with the chauffeur, a nephew, and a bodyguard, tried to leave. It took the pushing efforts of a dozen police who had been on guard duty to get the engine to run, and they finally got away. By the time Sasaki and his men arrived, all they could find out was that Suzuki was no longer there. A search verified that, so they set fire to the house, effectively this time, and left to go after the Privy Council head, Baron Hiranuma.

The Suzukis took shelter in the home of the Premier's sister in Hongo, but that didn't last very long. Hajime phoned the Suzuki residence at Maruyama to say they were safe at Hongo, but after saying it, realized he was probably talking to one of the rebellious soldiers, and hung up at once. The Suzukis decided they had better move on, once again, and finally came to rest in Shiba, at the home of some friends who lived next door to the Premier's brother, Gen. Takao Suzuki.

Captain Sasaki, that daring and intrepid patriot, having chased the aged premier and his wife from one place to another, found the big house of Baron Hiranuma and set it afire, hoping thus to get rid of another so-called traitor. This time the captain didn't check to see who was inside; he just started the fires, watched the house burn, and set out to return to Yokohama. It was full daylight, and getting too hot and bright to play with fire.

Baron Hiranuma, escaping through an unguarded gate, sat out the fire that destroyed his home in the library of a neighboring building. Suzuki and Hiranuma were targets, of one man who led a few others, not of a coordinated plot or conspiracy; but that, too, was taking place that night and early morning. It was a final, last-ditch effort to prevent the Emperor's wish for peace from coming about and to keep the Japanese people from hearing the Emperor's words.

The "Tokyo Rebellion" had a large cast, some of whom we've met before. They were generally people in important or key positions, and they had a power out of proportion to their numbers. As mentioned, there was a period in the twentieth century when, as an American observer commented, Japan was ruled by assassination. The killers were almost all reactionary military men who thought they knew best, and like spoiled children, had tantrums when crossed or opposed. Unlike an infant yelling or kicking his heels, though, these men took to the sword and gun, killing not only political opponents, but at times other military men who took a different view.

The older politicians in or out of power had all lived through at least one of these periods when the military ran wild. For many, like Suzuki, it had been a traumatic and nearly fatal experience. What the Army might do was on the minds of all the members of the Privy Council, the cabinet, and the *jushin*, as well as of the Emperor and his advisers. This was a part of the source of General Anami's power. It was believed that he could keep the Army in check. He was also feared, because he had the power to do what other military men had done in the past; for the sake of the Army, oppose the government and bring it down. It is to his credit that Anami, a stubborn and persevering but not necessarily brilliant man, evidently never considered taking such an action, although there was pressure brought on him to do so. He was a loyal and patriotic man, loyal to his Emperor, his country, and his service, and acted accordingly.

But even General Anami, despite the high regard his men held for him, had a tightrope to walk. He had to work out a way to hold his men's fealty while at the same time doing what was best for his country, what the Emperor wanted. It was not always easy. During this time he developed an affection for that old hero, Baron Suzuki, and an intense dislike for his opposite number, the Navy's Admiral Yonai. There seemed to be more than the traditional service rivalry behind this, although Anami was a very traditional man.

On the night of August 14, General Anami told his men, in effect, that though they might think losing the war was the end of the world, it wasn't; that they should stay proud to build a new and better Japan; that they should stay alive to help their Emperor and nation through this difficult time; that they should not obey the ancient warrior's code and kill themselves. Then, in the early morning of August 15, he returned home, went through the time-honored ritual, and did just that.

He had written out a message to the troops. It read in part:

The Emperor has made his decision. The Army expects you to obey that decision and make no unauthorized moves that would put to shame the glorious traditions of the Imperial Army and its many distinguished military services. You must behave in such a way that you need never fear the judgment of posterity, and it is expected that your conduct will enhance the honor and glory of the Imperial Japanese Forces in the eyes of the entire world.

The Minister of War and the Chief of Staff dispatch this order with grief in their hearts, and they expect you to appreciate the emotions of the Emperor when he himself broadcasts the Imperial Rescript terminating the war. . . .

That was an official duty. At his home, he brushed characters on two heavy sheets of paper. One said: "After tasting the profound benevolence of the Emperor, I have no words to speak." It was signed: "General Korechika. (The night of August 14th, 1945.)"

The other said: "For my supreme crime, I beg forgiveness through the act of death." This was signed: "Korechika Anami, Minister of War. (The night of August 14th, 1945.)"

To the above, he added: "I believe in Japan's sacred indestructibility."

It seemed that General Anami, as a person, was writing out a last word of respect for the Emperor; as War Minister, he was trying to take the responsibility for having lost the war. That would seem to be the supreme crime for which he wanted to be forgiven.

He spent his last hours drinking sake and talking to his brother-in-law, Lieutenant Colonel Takeshita, who had come to see him both to be with the Minister at a bitter time and to speak for his friend Major Hatanaka who wanted to get the Minister's approval of the revolt. Upon entering

General Anami's residence and taking one look at the Minister's face, Colonel Takeshita knew he was not going to bring up the revolt. As Anami continued his preparations and talks with his brother-in-law, he had another visitor, Colonel Ida, who had come to report to General Anami on the night's developments. When he realized what the War Minister was planning to do, he dropped the idea.

Anami had taken out two daggers, family heirlooms. He had handed one to Takeshita, asking him to take it as a keepsake. He had also asked Takeshita, in case he should fail in his attempt, to deliver the *coup de grace.* Then he had taken the second dagger, slashed himself across the stomach, and searching for the carotid artery, stabbed himself in the neck. More than an hour after the act, though bleeding profusely and unable to speak, he was still alive. Colonel Takeshita, mindful of his brother-in-law's last request and unwilling to see the suffering continue, picked up Anami's dagger from the floor and plunged it into the dying man's neck, bringing the episode and the War Minister's life to an end.

By this time it was bright daylight. Normal people in the capital, if there were any normal people that morning in Tokyo, were up and about, doing whatever they had to do, but scheduling themselves so as to be in front of a radio before noon. As with many events connected with the war in Japan, none of them knew what had been going on during the night. If they had, many would have been horrified; some would have applauded. All they knew was that rumors were flying around Tokyo like mad; but then, they always did.

There was a huge American task force just outside Tokyo Bay. The city, and country, would be invaded at any moment. The new type of bomb the news had mentioned as having been used at Hiroshima and Nagasaki was about to be used on Tokyo, and some survivors of the other two cities had reported that the only defense against the bomb was to be buried deep underground. The government was about to surrender, the Americans would come in and raze the country, the children would be killed, the men put to work as slaves, and the women systematically raped, so that there would soon be no more Japanese nation. Many of the military bases had refused to surrender, and the Army was in rebellion against halting the war.

Of all these, and other rumors, there was a slight bit of truth in the latter. There was a full-fledged, but poorly organized and somewhat disconnected, plot among some of the officers at the Ministry of War at Ichigaya Heights, the Tokyo version of the Pentagon. There were eight or ten officers who were determined to save their nation and Emperor from disgrace, whether or not either wanted to be so saved.

These men were, as a rule, the younger, up-and-coming officers, majors and colonels, not yet generals. Many of them had an exaggerated idea of their own importance and ability to sway the men under them. They also knew that they could not succeed without the tacit or expressed approval of a few key figures. As a result, as we have seen, they spent a certain amount of time and energy trying to get the consent of such men as Anami, Umezu, Yonai, and Toyoda. Failing to get their complete approval, there were some other officers who were necessary for their plans, men like General Mori of the Guards and General Tanaka of the Eastern District Army.

The Emperor had effectively neutralized many key men, such as Field Marshal Shunroku Hata, by getting statements of loyalty from them. But two of the leaders of the revolt were relatives of the really important men. Maj. Hidemasa Koga was the son-in-law of Gen. Hideki Tojo, the short, arrogant, bristling Premier at the time of Pearl Harbor, and Lt. Col. Masahiko Takeshita was General Anami's brother-in-law.

There were others, such as Lt. Col. Makoto Tsukamoto,

who played a peculiar role. Colonel Tsukamoto was an officer in the *Kempeitai*, the military police force considered to be the secret police. The *Kempeitai* was a semiautonomous organization, attached to no army and reporting directly to the Minister of War. The commandant of the organization called his officers together on August 14, told them of the Emperor's decision, and instructed his subordinates to obey the Imperial command. Despite this, it was reportedly a group of *Kempeitai* men who had gone after Marquis Kido and had had to be driven off by small arms fire.

Colonel Tsukamoto was an intelligent, sophisticated man. An undercover agent in China he had been working at his trade in Formosa when he suddenly received orders to report to Tokyo. He returned to the capital on August 6, but no one seemed to know why he had been sent for. However, his commandant, General Okida, assigned him to look into talk of a coup d'état or a revolt in the Army against "appeasers." On August 11, he found out why he had been recalled when he bumped into his old friend and companion Lt. Col. Masataka Ida of the War Ministry's Military Affairs Section. Colonel Ida had ordered Tsukamoto returned to Tokyo so that he could join the group of officers from the War Ministry who were going to rebel against acceptance of the Allied terms. Colonel Tsukamoto watched Colonel Ida and the plotters and reported rather noncommittally to General Okida while trying to make up his mind about the small group of plotters.

The plotters' plans changed with conditions. Originally, all they had wanted to do was show their objection to the surrender. Gradually, as conditions grew worse, the young officers grew more specific. As the chosen preservers of the national polity and Imperial institutions, they naturally had to remove from influence or the Emperor's immediate circle those traitorous, weak-minded advisers who were telling him to do the wrong things. Then, when it became obvious that these same traitorous advisers were winning the day, the rebels knew they would have to take stronger action. When the story got about that the Emperor was going to record or had recorded a speech announcing the end of the war, they had to keep the Japanese people from hearing this speech.

Probably the most intense of the plotters was Maj. Kenji Hatanaka of the Military Affairs Section, a pale, delicate young man who had been a special protégé of General Anami's. At one time or another, Hatanaka's path crossed that of the others at Ichigaya: Colonel Ida, Colonel Inaba, Major Ishihara, Major Koga, Colonel Shiizaki, and of course, Colonel Takeshita. The men were scurrying around Tokyo, the War Ministry, and the various Army headquarters, alternately depressed and hopeful but always busy as ants whose anthill has just been tipped over.

General Anami, knowing something of what was going on because of the attempts to get his backing for various plans for rebellion, gathered in his private office the big names of the military and had prepared a statement. It read: "The Imperial Forces will act strictly in accordance with the decision of His Imperial Majesty the Emperor." Anami was the first to sign it, followed by the Chief of Staff, the Director-General of Military Education, the Vice-Chief of Staff, the Vice-Minister of War, two Field Marshals, and various bureau, department, and section heads. This document, dated August 14, had the effect of spelling out the policy of the Imperial Army; those officers who did not follow that policy were not only insubordinate but guilty of treason.

Nevertheless, Hatanaka, Shiizaki, Ishihara, and Koga were meeting at the Imperial Guards' headquarters, trying to work out their plans. As a result, Major Hatanaka went to see Gen. Seiichi Tanaka, Commander of the Eastern District Army, whose job it was to defend Honshu and the Tokyo area. General Tanaka took one look at the excited major and stopped the younger man before he could speak. "I know what's on your mind," the general said. "I don't want to hear it. Leave at once."

Hatanaka tried to speak but couldn't. The initiative had been taken away from him. He saluted, turned on his heel, and left.

Colonel Ida had been lying down in the bomb shelter, thinking. There was no way out. When he came up, he saw a bonfire blazing on Ichigaya Hill, behind the War Ministry. The fire was gasoline-drenched paper, documents the Ministry was burning. When the fires ran low, soldiers brought more documents and threw them into the flames. Colonel Ida watched the fire with fascination, perhaps seeing it as symbolic of the Army and Japan. Then he told his fellow officers what he had been thinking and what he had decided: that he, and all of them, must commit seppuku; it was the only way they could apologize to the Emperor for the defeat.

A little later, while going through his effects in his room, preparing for his suicide, he was visited by the ubiquitous Colonel Hatanaka. The two men went to the top of the building and argued as to what was to be done. Colonel Ida tried to persuade Hatanaka that seppuku was the only honorable way out; Hatanaka wanted to lead an Army uprising. They parted with neither having convinced the other.

The protection of the Emperor was in the hands of three divisions of the Imperial Guards. The Second Division was serving overseas and the Third Division was attached to the Eastern Army, so the Palace was under the care of the First Division, whose two regiments alternated their guard duty. The regimental commander, Col. Toyojiro Haga, had ordered his adjutant, Capt. Otokichi Soga, to remain at division headquarters, a move which disconcerted the captain, who could see no reason for it. Nor could he see why there were two battalions there instead of the normal one. The extra men cluttered the Palace grounds.

Major Hatanaka was back in conference with the other

plotters. They were discussing the Imperial Guards, particularly Lieutenant Colonel Mizutani, the division's Chief of Staff, and Gen. Takeshi Mori, the division's commander. They knew they had to have these men on their side and were convinced that once they had Mori, Mizutani would follow. They figured that if they had the commanders of the first and second regiments, Mori would join with them. Then, in their dreams, all the Imperial Guards' officers would fall in line, as well as the heads of the Eastern District Army. The men went out to carry on their new duties, to speed up the revolt.

At about the same time, Captain Soga of the Second Infantry Regiment received a phone call from the Commander of the Fourth Regiment who reported that he had heard a rumor that an important division order was about to be issued that would be a forgery. Captain Soga, who knew nothing about this, tried to laugh it off, but he was disturbed enough to take a look around. All he could see were three unfamiliar officers at a Guards' command post, but as they were two lieutenant colonels and a major, it didn't strike him as worth investigating. Why should a captain start questioning his superiors?

A little later, Hatanaka and Shiizaki were closeted with Colonel Haga of the Second Regiment, trying to talk him into protecting the Emperor by isolating him from the traitors who were misadvising him. Haga was not impressed. Then they tried a hard sell, letting Haga in on the supposed news that the Minister of War, the Army Chief of Staff, the Commander of the Eastern District Army, and the Commander of the Imperial Guards' First Division were all in on the plan, intimating that this was Haga's big chance.

The fact that the four men they mentioned had all come out unequivocally against their plan seemed a minor detail to their inflamed minds, one not worth talking about.

Colonel Haga called in his adjutant, Captain Soga, and

told him to take down an order. The captain prepared to write it out. Haga seemed to be in deep thought, but he didn't speak. When he did, finally, he just said, "All right. You may go. I've changed my mind." After Soga left, Colonel Haga explained he hadn't changed his mind about joining them, but only about issuing the order, fearing it might be premature.

Hatanaka and Shiizaki then went to the War Ministry, where they found Colonel Ida asleep in a room he'd been using. The two men awakened him and told him they wanted his approval for a plan. Shiizaka said that Ida had turned down Hatanaka that afternoon; now he had come to make another request for approval. Hatanaka explained that now the Imperial Guards were with them, except for General Mori, and that Colonel Ida was the man to convince him to come on. General Mori had been one of Hatanaka's teachers at War College and still thought of him as immature, and Colonel Kaga was also too young to impress the general. But if Colonel Ida would talk to General Mori for them, the general would certainly come around.

"But if he doesn't?" Colonel Ida asked.

Then, Hatanaka said, they would just have to accept that as a fact. "I promise on my word of honor to forget the whole thing if the Lieutenant Colonel fails to persuade General Mori," Hatanaka said.

Hatanaka, Shiizaki, and Ida set off for the Imperial Guards' headquarters to see General Mori, who was tied up at a conference. They sat in the staff room, along with Major Koga, Major Ishihara, and Capt. Shigetaro Uehara, of the Air Academy, and discussed their plan. Koga and Ishihara were pleased to hear Hatanaka report that the Guards' battalion heads had not only agreed to cooperate but had already stationed troops at strategic spots around the Palace. But they all knew that General Mori was the fulcrum on which the plan now rested. If he refused to cooperate, the whole scheme might well blow up. Already almost midnight, it looked as though a new day was about to start with the rebellion no further along. And time was running out, as they all knew.

Hatanaka, the most volatile and impatient of the "patriots," had been pacing back and forth, muttering about the lack of time. Suddenly remembering something he had to do, he left with Captain Uehara. At about 12:30, General Mori's visitor, his brother-in-law, Lt. Col. Michinori Shiraishi, a staff officer of the Second Army stationed at Hiroshima, had finished his visit. General Mori sent out word that he could now receive the officers. By now they were reduced to two, Colonels Ida and Shiizaki. Ida, who had been planning seppuku, felt that Hatanaka had let him down by disappearing, but went in to try to present Hatanaka's case to General Mori, who sat at his desk with Colonel Shiraishi standing behind him.

General Mori must have known what the officers had in mind. He spent the next fifteen minutes politely keeping them from speaking, quietly explaining to them his philosophy of life and the war. The room was small and very hot, and Ida was getting impatient and tense. It was a donnish type of lecture, and Colonel Ida could understand how General Mori got the nickname "Monk." Whenever Ida tried to break in, in the usual polite Japanese fashion, General Mori would ask him to wait and would go on with his explanation of his views.

Finally, Colonel Ida had a chance to speak, and picking up the other man's mood, expressed his views about the natural unity of the Emperor and his subjects. Colonel Ida was passing along, more or less, the theories of Kiyoshi Hiraizumi, a professor at Tokyo University whose lectures at the War College on the divinity of the Emperor and the indivisibility of the people, the country, and the Emperor had made quite an impression on the young officers.

General Mori listened politely and then said that whatever the merit of Ida's argument, the fact remained that the Emperor had spoken, and as commander of the Imperial Guards, he must obey that decision and insist that his men obey it. Colonel Ida countered with familiar arguments about Japan's sacredness and indestructibility. General Mori said he understood and sympathized with the other man's views, but he was sworn to abide by the Emperor's decision. However, he went on, his intention now was to go to the Meiji Shrine and pray.

At this point, Col. Kazuo Mizutani, the division's Chief of Staff, looked in at Mori's office and started to leave. Mori asked him to listen to Colonel Ida, and Mizutani said he would go to his office. General Mori suggested that Colonel Ida get Colonel Mizutani's views. As Ida was leaving General Mori's office, Hatanaka and Uehara rushed in. Colonel Ida smiled at them and told them to wait in Mori's office while he spoke to Mizutani. Ida, feeling calmer now, had started to explain his view of the situation to Mizutani when a shot rang out.

The two men jumped up and ran for the next office, from which the shot had come. As they reached the corridor, the door to Mori's office opened and Hatanaka came out, a smoking pistol in his hand. "There was no time," he said. "No time to argue, so I killed him. What else could I do?"

Ida and Mizutani looked into the general's office. Captain Uehara was wiping his bloody sword; Shiizaki was sitting in a chair, dazed. On the floor lay the hacked and lifeless bodies of General Mori and his brother-in-law, Colonel Shiraishi.

Hatanaka and Uehara saluted the dead bodies and got back to work. Their schedule had set the time for the uprising at 0200. The two conspirators didn't stop to think that the assassination of General Mori might have made their whole plan completely unworkable. Colonel Ida, probably shocked out of his normal senses, saw things the same way. He said he

was going to the Eastern District Army Headquarters, and
Hatanaka agreed. Ida and Mizutani got into a staff car and
left.

Hatanaka, when he had first left General Mori's office, had
gone to Colonel Takeshita's office and, talking to him in his
wild fashion, had convinced the colonel to go visit his father-
in-law Anami and persuade him to join in the coup. Now,
things were different.

Hatanaka by now was deeply and emotionally committed
to his plan. He looked at a document that Major Koga and
Major Ishihara had drawn up.

IMPERIAL GUARDS DIVISION STRATEGIC ORDER #584

Date: Aug. 15, 1945

Time: 0200

1. The Division will defeat the enemy's scheme; it will protect
the Emperor and preserve the national polity.

2. The commander of the First Infantry Regiment will occupy
the East Second and East Third garrison grounds (including the
surroundings of the Eastern District Army strategy room) and the
environs of Honmaru Baba, thus guarding the Imperial Family
from this sector. The commander will also order a company to
occupy the Tokyo Broadcasting Station and prohibit all broadcasts.

3. The commander of the Second Infantry Regiment will use
his main force to guard the Imperial Family at the Fukiage district of the Imperial Palace.

4. The commander of the Sixth Infantry Regiment will continue present duties.

5. The commander of the Seventh Infantry Regiment will
occupy the area of Nijubashi Gate and prevent any contact with
the Imperial Palace.

6. The commander of the Cavalry Regiment will order a tank
force to Daikan Avenue to await further orders.

7. The commander of the First Artillery Regiment will await
further orders.

8. The commander of the First Engineers will await further orders.

9. The commander of the Mechanized Battalion will guard the Imperial Palace at its present strength.

10. The commander of the Signal Unit will sever all communication with the Imperial Palace except through Division Headquarters.

11. I shall be at Division Headquarters.

Hatanaka, looking through General Mori's desk, found the dead man's private seal, which he ordered affixed to copies of the order. These were sent by messengers to the officers involved. Hatanaka thought that if Colonel Ida succeeded with the Eastern Army, and Takeshita with Anami, his plan would succeed. Now it was time for his next step.

Major Hatanaka and Colonel Shiizaki, who during the day had been furiously and dustily and sweatily bicycling from place to place, now got into a staff car bearing the insignia of the First Imperial Guards Division and had themselves driven to the Imperial Palace grounds. Going first to the headquarters of the Second Regiment, they told Haga that they had been appointed staff officers of the Imperial Guards Division to make sure that special orders for the security of the Imperial Palace were carried out. As Major Hatanaka was saying this, an adjutant arrived, as though on cue, and handed the forged orders to Haga.

Haga knew there was talk of insurrection. It did not occur to him that he was part of a revolt against the Army. He acted as instructed and took the necessary steps to quarantine the Palace.

At Eastern District Army Headquarters, things seemed very quiet in the early morning hours. The quiet was interrupted by a phone call, answered by Lt. Col. Hiroshi Fuha, a staff officer. The voice on the other end was excited, nearly hysterical; it was the voice of Major Koga. Koga said the Guards refused to accept the surrender and wanted to know whether the Eastern Army would join in the revolt. The question was repeated, and then the conversation ended.

Fuha connected the call with rumors he had heard about a possible Army revolt, but the phone conversation still seemed unlikely—he, himself, had heard the commander of the Eastern Army, General Tanaka, angrily refuse to discuss the subject, and he had heard General Mori say he would obey the Emperor's decision. Nevertheless, he felt he should inform General Tanaka of the call. When he entered the office, he found General Tanaka talking to his Chief of Staff, Maj. Gen. Tatsuhiko Takashima. The two generals listened, but took no action; they knew General Mori wouldn't allow any nonsense in his Guards Division.

General Takashima had just returned to his office when two officers came in, Colonel Ida and Colonel Mizutani, both obviously excited. It was Mizutani who found his voice first. "Mori has been murdered," he said. "The Guards are occupying the Palace. I've come to Eastern Army for instructions. . . ." And then he fainted.

General Takashima had some men tend to Mizutani and asked Colonel Ida for an explanation. Ida, though he knew better, went into his spiel about an uprising, pressure to save the Emperor, peace with honor, etc. Takashima asked what Ida wanted the Eastern Army to do. He was told they should approve the action of the Guards and send some men to join them. General Takashima said there was nothing he could do without an order from General Tanaka and left Colonel Ida with Colonel Itagaki while he went to find his commander.

General Tanaka decided to go to the Palace at once, as soon as he had heard the story, but Takashima urged him to wait until they were in a better position to know just which officers were involved and what they had done. General Takashima went back to the staff room and ordered a number of his officers to be alert for further information. Colonel

Itagaki had persuaded Colonel Ida to return to the Imperial Palace and, as a friend of Hatanaka's, to persuade him to stop the revolt.

Colonel Itagaki and Colonel Fuha went to Guards head-quarters to investigate further. They found the Palace in darkness, as an air-raid warning was in effect. Although they were halted a number of times, no one stopped them for good because they were staff officers. Eventually they reached the staff room where they found a young officer. It was Sadakichi Ishihara, a Guards staff officer and one of the leaders of the rebellion, who was maintaining the contact of the division with the rest of the world. The two colonels tried to find out what was going on but received no satisfactory information. Their mission, however, had been to discover the truth about the death of General Mori. When they tried to enter his office, a sentry refused them entrance, but Major Ishihara, who had followed them, had them admitted.

The bodies of General Mori and Colonel Shiraishi were still there, as they had been left. It was a shocking scene, even in wartime, and it left the two colonels stunned. There was an element of violent brutality about these deaths; they were not so much cold-blooded assassinations as acts of rage, a venting of frustrations and hostilities. Although the men were no more or less dead than they would have been had each been the victim of one well-placed shot, this seemed more shocking, and more reprehensible.

The two officers tore themselves away from the grisly sight, and returned to Eastern Army Headquarters to report to General Takashima, who in turn reported their findings to General Tanaka. It was felt that the most important thing now was to reach Colonel Haga, Second Regiment com-mander, who had been having his own doubts. He had been told by Major Hatanaka that General Anami was on his way to the Palace to persuade the Emperor to change his position

and that General Mori was in sympathy with the rebellion
and was about to issue revised orders. That had been several
hours earlier, soon after midnight.

Colonel Haga questioned Hatanaka again, asking where
Anami was and wanting to know what had gone wrong.
Hatanaka said he would phone the War Minister to find out
whether he was on the way. At this point, Major Koga
returned. He saw that Colonel Haga was becoming restive
and probably could not be stalled any longer. He told Haga
that General Mori was dead and that he, Colonel Haga, must
take command of the Guards division. Haga demurred, asking
why it should be he and not Colonel Mizutani. Koga said the
Chief of Staff was at Eastern Army Headquarters trying to
persuade them to join the rebellion. Haga asked how
General Mori had died, but received no satisfactory answer.

General Takashima had been trying to reach Colonel Haga
on the phone ever since he'd received the reports confirming
General Mori's death. He finally got through to him on a
connection so bad that neither man could hear clearly. General Takashima kept repeating that the division order with
Mori's seal and signature was a forgery, that the troops
around the Palace must be dispersed, and that Haga should
send to Eastern District Army Headquarters for new orders.
Takashima repeated this until he was convinced that Colonel
Haga understood him. Even with the bad connection, something made him realize that Colonel Haga was not alone.
When he asked whether anyone else was there, the colonel
said that Hatanaka was standing next to him.

Hatanaka spent some time, despite the poor connection,
trying to explain his position to Takashima and got nowhere.
Takashima told him that his position was hopeless and that
he must obey the Emperor. Hatanaka asked for one thing:
Before the Emperor's speech could be broadcast, he wanted
ten minutes to talk to the Japanese people, ten minutes in
which to explain the rebels' reasons for their actions and the

goals they hoped to win. Takashima said there was no hope at all for the rebels, that the only thing to do now was to make certain there were no more unnecessary deaths.

Colonel Haga, of course, had heard one half of the conversation. He spoke angrily to Hatanaka, saying he'd been lying the whole time, that this was a rebellion, and that he, Colonel Haga, wanted no part of it. He ended by ordering Major Hatanaka to leave the Palace grounds. Major Hatanaka then left for the NHK studios, a mile and a half away.

The First Regiment of the Imperial Guards had surrounded the building and had posted soldiers at all entrances. Major Koga's falsely signed order had gone into effect. The broadcasting rooms had been closed to all outsiders, and some sixty NHK employees had been locked into a big studio.

It was a little before five when Major Hatanaka, escorted by a lieutenant and two privates, arrived. Hatanaka, showing a pistol, insisted that he wanted to take over the five o'clock news broadcast. An announcer said that it couldn't be done, using as a reason the fact that an air-raid warning was still in effect and insisting that they would have to get special permission to break this from the Eastern Army. Hatanaka, knowing that permission would never be given, continued arguing.

For an hour, Major Hatanaka put on a one-man show at NHK, a show that didn't get on the air. He waved his pistol recklessly and talked wildly about what he would do to the people who wouldn't let him explain his actions and reasons to the people of Japan. But he didn't get anywhere.

Even if he had seized a microphone and tried to broadcast, his speech wouldn't have gone out, as the radio people had disconnected the line between their building and the transmitting tower. He finally got an opportunity to state his case, into a telephone. He had been interrupted in his ranting by a telephone call from a general staff officer of the Eastern

District Army. Hatanaka repeated all the arguments he had used about honor, Japan, and continuing the war, but he seemed to be only going through the motions. Finally he hung up, a defeated man, gathered his escort together, and left the building as suddenly and as rudely as he had come. The NHK staff went back to their work of preparing for the Emperor's broadcast.

In midmorning, Colonel Tsukamoto, the *Kempeitai* agent who had been recalled from Formosa, received word from one of his men that two officers, one on horseback, the other riding a motorcycle, were outside the Imperial Palace, handing out leaflets urging the populace not to accept the surrender but to go on fighting. Tsukamoto, who remembered Hatanaka and Shiizaki, figured it was they. He sent a man to the Palace grounds to put the two men under guard.

Major Hatanaka was on the motorcycle; Colonel Shiizaki riding his horse. They were handing out leaflets which read:

We the officers of the Imperial Japanese Army, who, this morning of August 15, 1945, have risen up in arms, declare to all officers and soldiers of the Armed Forces and to the Japanese people:

That our intention is to protect the Emperor and to preserve the national polity despite the designs of the enemy;

That our prime concern is neither victory nor defeat; nor are we motivated by selfish interests;

That we are ready to live, or die, for the sole just and righteous cause of national loyalty; and

That we devoutly pray that the Japanese people and the members of the Armed Forces will appreciate the significance of our action and join with us to fight for the preservation of our country and the elimination of the traitors around the Emperor, thus confounding the schemes of the enemy.

Hatanaka was finally getting his message across to the people. The leaflets were thrust into the hands of passersby who looked at the messages, threw them away, and passed by.

CHAPTER IX

"The Guards Are Occupying the Palace"

It is possible that Hatanaka and his group might have been able to put their case before the Japanese public if they hadn't made a major strategic error. By taking over the Palace grounds in an attempt to keep the Emperor's recorded speech from being broadcast, they were, in fact as well as theory, moving against the Emperor. They were so frightened of the effect of a direct talk to the people by this small, mild, shy man that they ended by gaining the opposition of the people they needed most and who were most in sympathy with their ideals—the established militarists. Like fanatics everywhere, they became victims of their own propaganda. They were so imbued with the righteousness of their cause that they thought everyone must see it the same way and that those who didn't either hadn't understood or were traitors.

Most of the men around the Emperor, his chamberlains and other civilians and aides, had heard rumors about a possible Army coup. They didn't discount these stories, for they knew this was a possibility and one that they feared. But they did not feel it would be directed in any way against the Emperor. Even General Mori, when he was questioned about the Imperial Guards by General Hasunuma, the Emperor's chief aide-de-camp, said that although they were a little restless, he wasn't worried about them, that stories about possible defections were only rumors.

Marquis Kido felt somewhat the same way. Having been alerted to the rumors by Prince Konoye, he informed Premier Suzuki of them. Suzuki said he had heard nothing but even without General Mori's words, the Imperial Guards were the last people he would worry about.

As it turned out, General Mori was certainly loyal to the Emperor, loyal to the end, which came unexpectedly for him. Except for a few officers, the Guards were loyal, too. Even when they followed the wrong course of action, it was not out of any desire to lead or be part of a rebellion. They thought they were doing their duty—protecting the Emperor. They were following their commander's orders; they had no way of knowing their commander was dead, the orders false.

By 2:00 A.M., the rebels' audacious plan seemed to have worked. The Imperial Palace was entirely in their hands: The Palace police had been disarmed, the grounds surrounded, all entrances blocked and almost all communication with the outside world broken. But the Emperor and his family and his chamberlains were unaware that they were prisoners, that any of these things had happened.

Information Director Shimomura, having completed his task—seeing that the recordings of the Emperor's speech were safely in the care of the Imperial Chamberlain—figured he should report to the Prime Minister, and with his secretary, Nobumasa Kawamoto, started by car for the Premier's official residence. The car was stopped by a soldier who asked whether he was the Director of the Information Bureau. When the answer was yes, soldiers jumped on the running boards and ordered the car back. Shimomura, his secretary, his bodyguard, and his chauffeur were taken from the car and put into a small, bare Army barracks, about fifteen feet by twelve.

They were soon joined by the three top men of the Japan Broadcasting Corporation, and the recording team, all of whom had been intercepted as they tried to leave the Palace grounds after making the recordings at the Household Ministry. Eventually, sixteen men were crowded in there, and for some time not allowed to talk, not allowed to smoke, and not allowed to sit down. The windows were closed and covered, and the room became a hot box. Eventually after a list was made of who and what the prisoners were, the rules were relaxed a bit. Although they still could not take off their coats, talk to one another, or smoke, they were allowed to sit down—those who could find a place to sit.

Not too far from them, inside the grounds, three of the Emperor's chamberlains were having a quiet meeting while waiting for the air-raid alert to end. There hadn't been a plane attacking Tokyo, but nearby Kumagaya was burning. While waiting for the all-clear, Yasuhide Toda, Yasuya Mitsui, and Yoshihiro Tokugawa discussed the long day's events, glad that the day was over and that the recording was safely stowed away. They obviously didn't know that the Palace was encircled.

However, Sotaro Ishiwatari, the Imperial Household Minister, must have realized that something was amiss, as he had been stopped when he tried to leave the Palace, but had been allowed to return to the Ministry. These were peculiar times, to be sure. Beginning to worry about Shimomura and the others who had left earlier, he asked Susumu Kato, head of the Household Ministry's General Affairs Bureau, to check. Kato and one of the Ministry police went to the Guards' command post. In a few minutes, the little barracks' population increased by two, making eighteen.

Major Hatanaka, having ordered light machine guns

placed at every entrance to the Palace, began questioning his
prisoners, starting with Kato, trying to find out where the
Household Minister and Marquis Kido were. Kato couldn't
tell him, and Hatanaka was no more successful getting the
information out of the others. All he could find out was that
the Emperor had made a recording, but not one of the
prisoners seemed to know where it was.

While this was going on, four men, the Minister Ishiwatari,
Ogane, the Vice-Minister, Section Chief Kakei, and the Minister's secretary, Ishikawa, sat around a telephone in the
underground shelter of the Household Ministry. The Minister was trying to reach General Mori to tell him that Kato
was missing and that he was also worried about Shimomura
and others. But the phone calls were unsatisfactory. When
there was an answer, the man at the other end wouldn't
identify himself nor would he connect him with Mori.

The telephoning stopped soon when a group of soldiers
came into the room. The officer in charge said, "Orders,"
and the men chopped through the telephone lines with fire
axes, and left.

In another part of the Palace, Chamberlain Mitsui was
awakened in the dark by the voice of Vice-Minister Ogane,
whispering that the Imperial Guards had occupied the Palace
and cut all the telephone wires. Mitsui thought he should
tell Chamberlain Toda, but just then Toda came into the
room, having heard Ogane's whisper. Mitsui then thought
he should warn the others. Making his way through the dark
corridors to Chamberlain Tokugawa's bedroom, he awakened him, told him, and went on to the small bedroom of
two aides-de-camp. These two went to Chief Aide-de-Camp
Hasunuma. They went to their office to telephone, but the
phone was dead. It was just 0300.

Chamberlain Tokugawa took the Household Minister and
his two secretaries and police guards upstairs to an anteroom
used by the ladies-in-waiting. There was a cupboard which,

when opened, revealed a hidden passage to an underground room the chamberlains called the bank vault. A little later, Chamberlain Toda moved Marquis Kido from his own room to the doctor's office, and then later with Tokugawa, to the "bank vault" with the others.

Whether the insurgents' main goal was to take over the Palace, cut off the Emperor from outside contact, and then force a change of mind, or to prevent the Emperor's war-ending broadcast from being made is a question that can never be settled. Of course, being able to force the Emperor to change his mind was dependent on being able to keep the broadcast from being heard. But if that was the main purpose, why was the search for the recording entrusted to underlings, rather than to the officers leading the uprising?

In addition to the recording, there were two men the rebels particularly wanted to find—the Imperial Household Minister, Ishiwatari, and Marquis Kido—because the rebellious officers thought these two would know where the recording was.

Major Koga, who by now had a list of names and positions of the men held in the little barracks, had Kenjiro Yabe, Director of NHK's Domestic Bureau, brought to him for questioning. Koga asked Yabe a number of questions, but ascertained only that a satisfactory recording had been made, that it was in the Imperial Household Ministry, and that it would be broadcast at noon, or in about eight and a half hours. Major Koga called in another officer to take Yabe to the Household Ministry to make a search for the recording.

The search was fairly thorough and quite fruitless. The problem was compounded by the total unfamiliarity of almost all the searchers with the grounds and buildings. The Household Ministry consisted of several buildings grouped around a main office building. The buildings were full of corridors which passed hundreds of small cubicles, all of which looked alike, many identified by names that meant nothing to the searchers, nor did they have any idea which rooms were used by whom. To add to the confusion, the Ministry personnel, from the Minister to lowly clerks (including Imperial chamberlains), wore the same simple blue wartime uniforms, with the marks of rank being hard to identify. In addition to being unable to distinguish one room from the next, the soldiers couldn't tell one person from another.

Nor did they realize that because of wartime dislocations, some cupboards and cabinets normally used for the storage of bedding now hid valuable documents. One of the main buildings was on the side of a hill, so that the soldiers who entered from the front were on the first floor whereas those who came in from the rear found themselves on the third. In addition, because of the blackout, they were operating in these strange surroundings in almost total darkness, having to use flashlights except where they could turn on a light in a dark-curtained room.

The soldiers, accustomed to getting what they wanted without too much trouble from the civilian population and officials, found these conditions almost entirely frustrating, a feeling no doubt magnified by the impassive, detached attitude of the chamberlains and other staff members they confronted. Whether the Imperial staff meant to or not, they succeeded in making the soldiers feel ill-bred, uncouth, and rough. And soon, out of sheer frustration or for other reasons, they lost any semblance of politeness or respect. They no longer slid open the doors, they kicked them in with their booots; they made no attempt to sort through things to look for the recordings, they opened drawers and turned them upside down on the floor. Soon the areas through which they had searched looked more as though they had been looted by vandals than as though the Imperial Guards had been there.

By this time it was obvious to two chamberlains, Toda and Tokugawa, that the insurgents were not going to be successful in their search, so they decided they should try to warn the Emperor. Making it to a gate, they identified themselves as Imperial chamberlains with business at the Gobunko. The soldiers on guard there hesitated a moment, and then stepped aside. The Gobunko, the former library which was now serving as the Emperor's living quarters and office, was as dark as the rest of Tokyo. Passing through the east entrance, Tokugawa and Toda saw Chamberlain Irie asleep at his duty post. Their first reaction was one of relief that all was quiet near the Emperor; their next one was outrage. How could Irie sleep with all the terrible things going on so close by? They awakened him.

Chamberlain Irie, having been told the story, took them to Chamberlain Nagazumi, who was on duty near the Emperor's bed chamber, and then to Takeko Hoshina, the principal lady-in-waiting. They informed them of the events, saying there was no need to awaken the Emperor now, but to make sure to tell him when he awoke.

Then they decided to batten down the Gobunko, to see that all the doors were barred and the iron shutters over the windows fastened. The doors were no problem, but the shutters had not been used for so long that they were rusted, and the chamberlains had to get the help of some sturdy young guards. Chamberlain Irie, watching them go around the building barring the windows, thought how strange it was that the windows in the Imperial Palace were being shuttered, not against possible assault by enemy troops, but against soldiers of Japan, and to make it worse, against the Imperial Guards.

Tokugawa and Toda returned to the Household Ministry, able to report that all was well at the Gobunko. Toda reported to the chamberlains, and Tokugawa, to the aides-de-camp. After leaving them, Tokugawa was stopped by a soldier who ordered a guard to bring the chamberlain along. Tokugawa refused, saying that he didn't have to go anywhere with the soldier, that any questions could be asked where they were, which happened to be directly below the room where the Emperor's recording had been made. Several officers and enlisted men were running up and down the stairs —the search for the wanted recording had become increasingly frenetic with their repeated failures to find it or get information leading to it.

The soldier said they were looking for the Emperor's recording and for Marquis Kido. Tokugawa asked how he could be expected to know where they were, which provoked a chorus of "kill him" from some other officers who had stopped to listen. Tokugawa told them to go ahead and kill him, but they wouldn't gain by that. The others departed to continue their search, leaving Tokugawa arguing with the young soldier who had stopped him and listening to the familiar arguments about doing this for the Emperor's good so that the old, true Japanese order could be restored. Tokugawa answered angrily that he, too, was trying to do his job, to serve the Emperor. For his pains, the soldier punched him in the face, knocking him down.

Not long after this incident, Chamberlain Tokugawa had his spirits lifted. A naval aide-de-camp had discovered one phone line that had not been cut, a direct line to the Navy Ministry. Using it, he reported that General Mori had been murdered and the Palace occupied by Imperial Guards. The lieutenant commander on duty at the Navy Ministry promised immediate relief. That was shortly before 5:00 A.M.

Hearing that relief should be on the way, Chamberlain Toda once again made his way through the Guards to the Gobunko to pass on the information. He reported to Hisanori Fujita, the Grand Chamberlain, and soon there was a general discussion going on among several chamberlains and the Emperor's Steward as to whether they should attempt to hold the Gobunko if the insurgents should try to enter. The chief Gobunko guard, who had gone out a little earlier to confront the Guards, had not yet returned; they were afraid he had been captured or killed.

With no armed guards or police to help them, they tried to concoct a plan to spare the Emperor's living quarters from the desecration of violence. The Gobunko, with all doors and windows closed and barred, was a depressing and silent place now, dark except for the electric lights in shuttered rooms that were being used. The chamberlains decided that when the soldiers came hammering at the door, they would let them in and take them on a conducted tour of the Gobunko, which would give the Emperor and Empress a chance to escape. They didn't think it was a very good plan, but they hadn't been able to come up with a better one.

They also decided, without enthusiasm, that if that were the plan, it was time to awaken the Emperor and tell him about it. Chamberlains Toda and Mitsui were given the unwelcome task. The Emperor made it as easy for them as possible, asking a few questions, then requesting that the Imperial Guards be gathered together in the garden so that he could explain his decision to them. The Emperor wished the chief aide-de-camp to be called, which wasn't as simple as it sounded since Hasunuma was in the Imperial Household Ministry, separated from them by some distance and a number of armed and hostile soldiers. Mitsui, as head of the General Affairs Section, unhappily started toward the Household Ministry buildings.

A few minutes earlier, at 5:10 A.M., General Tanaka, Commander of the Eastern District Army, arrived at Guards' headquarters, accompanied by his adjutant and a staff officer, Lieutenant Colonel Fuha. A complement of the First Guards Regiment, under the command of Colonel Watanabe, was just about to set out for the Imperial Palace, acting under Division Order #584. About the last person Colonel Watanabe expected to see that early morning was the high-ranking

General Tanaka, and he hurried over to escort his unanticipated visitor into his own office.

The Eastern Army Commander explained to Watanabe that General Mori had been murdered and that the orders under which he was about to act were false. Watanabe said the orders had been given to him by Major Ishihara who was nearby. General Tanaka ordered Ishihara in and told the Guards' officer that he considered his acting against the command of the Emperor a matter of high treason. He then had Ishihara put under guard and handed over to a *Kempeitai* sergeant.

General Tanaka was able to get in touch with Colonel Haga, Commander of the Second Imperial Guards Regiment, and told him that the men should be returned to their original stations, and that he, General Tanaka, was now in command of the Imperial Guards. Then as the general started toward the Gobunko to tell the Emperor what had happened, he saw an Imperial chamberlain coming toward him.

Tanaka asked whether the Grand Chamberlain or Chief Aide-de-Camp was at the Gobunko and was told no. He asked whether the Emperor could be found there and heard that the Emperor was there.

General Tanaka, seeing that the chamberlain was troubled, realized the cause of his worry. "The revolt is over," he said, and extended his card. Mitsui, the chamberlain, did the same. The two men bowed to each other, read the cards, and bowed again. General Tanaka said he found it strange that neither the Grand Chamberlain nor the Chief Aide-de-Camp was with the Emperor. To this, Mitsui admitted that the Grand Chamberlain was, and that he, himself, was on his way to the Ministry to summon the other to the Gobunko.

Tanaka continued on his way; in time, he was able to see the Grand Chamberlain to ask him to convey to the

Emperor his most profound apologies and sorrow at any discomfort his delay may have caused.

The men who had been locked in the sweltering barracks since early morning were suddenly let out, without any explanation, just a corporal's apology for having delayed them so long. Soon after that, Chamberlain Mitsui made his way to the "bank vault" and pounded on the heavy iron door until he identified himself. When it was finally opened, he told the men inside that it was now safe for them to come out.

At 0721, NHK made a special announcement that it repeated at intervals for the next few hours: "His Imperial Majesty has issued a rescript. It will be broadcast at noon today. Let us all respectfully listen to the voice of the Emperor."

At noon, an announcer said: "A broadcast of the highest importance is about to be made. All listeners will please rise."

The nation rose.

The announcer spoke again: "His Majesty, the Emperor, will now read his Imperial rescript to the people of Japan. We respectfully transmit his voice."

The announcer's solemn words were followed by the sound of "Kimigayo," the Japanese national anthem.

There was a moment of silence after the music died away. And then, "To our good and loyal subjects. . . ."

CHAPTER X

After the Last Battle

The effect of the Emperor's broadcast to the people of Japan can hardly be overestimated. It was, for the highly traditional Japanese, a major breakthrough in the Imperial tradition. But it was a critical situation, and emergency measures were necessary.

One of the reasons for the speech, as we have seen, was to acquaint the people with the fact that they had lost the war and that their land was about to be occupied by the enemy. The other was an attempt to ensure the laying down of arms by the military, of whom several million men were not in Japan proper. Realizing the extent of this problem, the Emperor had indicated his willingness to go talk to troops overseas. It was also suggested that other members of the Imperial family carry the message to the overseas contingents.

There were many reasons for this, one being the reiterated notion that the Japanese military had no word in their lexicon for *surrender*. Another was the matter of saving face, which was more serious than a mere wound to *amour-propre*. There were Japanese troops abroad, ranging from the high-

est officers to the lowest clerks, who were afraid to go home
—afraid that as losers they woud be held in such scorn that
their lives would not be worth living, afraid they would
have to commit seppuku, or at least be expected to.

For the Japanese, a whole generation had grown up under
war conditions, since the Manchurian incident in 1931.
The war had been a series of glorious victories for the Japanese people until 1942 and had not been brought home to
them in all its horror until 1944. Over a period of time, the
military had built up its own empire and empires, starting
in Manchuria and extending through the Pacific. It was
difficult, seemingly impossible, for some of the commanders
to realize that these were now lost.

There were many stories, some of them authentic, of Japanese garrisons on out-of-the-way islands who did not hear
the news that the war was over, or who did not believe it
when they heard it, and continued hiding and living in fear.

In Japan, the people as a whole were overwhelmed that
the Emperor would speak to them. Even though only a short
time was available to notify the populace of the speech, it
was heard by practically everyone on the home islands. Radio
had been a main means of communication for the Japanese
during the war, but by 1945, shortages in Japan had resulted
in broadcasts being sharply reduced. There were not enough
vacuum tubes necessary for transmitters and receivers, and
there was a chronic power shortage.

However, on August 15, NHK restored its power to prewar levels for a brief time, and cities and towns and hamlets,
which were accustomed to having very little or no electric
power at various times of the day, were assured of a full
supply so that everyone, everywhere, could listen. Before
noon, business, traffic, and conversation stopped completely,
and the strains of "Kimigayo" could be heard everywhere.

It was a highly emotional time for the people, not only
because it signified the end of what had turned into a ghastly,

losing war, but because it was, in its way, an emotional speech, a call to the people to face new hardships and to work together to surmount them. But the greatest appeal was that it was actually the Emperor himself speaking to them. The nation seemed to dissolve in sobs, young and old, sentimental and hard-bitten.

The people wept because it was the Emperor who was taking the time and trouble to talk to them, to console them, taking them into his confidence. They wept despite the fact that they did not understand all that he was saying; in fact, many understood very little because the Emperor's speech was written, quite naturally, in what might be called Court Japanese. This is an esoteric language using formal, old-fashioned, archaic terms and forms, and as the Japanese language is famous for its delicacy of phrasing and fine shadings of meanings, this was a complication. The men who wrote the draft of the rescript had been forced to check into many sources to be sure the formal style they were using was correct.

The style, however, didn't matter, except to the purists, because the people were listening to find out, not each possibly subtle meaning in every sentence, but the overall feeling of their Emperor. They listened to the speech alone, in families, in groups, in homes, in public squares, in private and public buildings, in a silence that was broken only by the sound of weeping. And they found out what they wanted to know—the Emperor was talking to them because he cared for them, cared about their losses and hardships and troubles. And that was all they wanted to know.

The Emperor was not a good speaker. In addition to being naturally shy and retiring, his style of life and training had not equipped him for public speaking. His voice was rather reedy, and he was nervous. In addition, he was very upset himself, and was fighting against it in order to uphold the unemotional tradition expected of him. From the stand-point of oratory, the broadcast was nothing special; from other points of view, it was a great success. The thought and feeling of the Emperor came through to his people who desperately needed something to help them through the next days and weeks and months.

It was unprecedented, as were his talks to the Supreme Council and the cabinet. Like them, it seemed to be the last word. But, as was the case when he finished those talks, there were still some who talked and took action afterwards.

The Emperor and his advisers were afraid of a wave of suicides following the rescript. These suicides would be according to the code, which required seppuku, or hara-kiri, to atone for loss of face. General Anami had cautioned his men against it in no uncertain terms, pointing out that they had to live to help rebuild Japan. It did not seem in-consistent to his officers that he killed himself; many of them felt he was doing it for them.

Despite the advice against it, there were many suicides. The war was over, the conquerors were coming, Japan would never be the same. Many people felt they should do this as a gesture for the Emperor, and the grounds in front of the Palace became a popular place to commit seppuku, either in the traditional way or in a more modern fashion, with a gun.

In the afternoon following the broadcast of the rescript, residents of Tokyo congregated in front of the Palace to show their continued allegiance to the Emperor. Many were crying as they bowed and prayed. Scattered among the crowd were Army officers who had come to pay their last respects. Mingled with other crowd noises were pistol shots as these men performed the act for which they had come and toppled to the ground. The others simply moved away from them, perhaps feeling it was their business, their right.

Major Koga, who had not been among the most moderate of men, was reportedly disturbed by the murder of General Mori. Koga had known that if the rebellion failed, he would kill himself, but he chose to do it at the Guards' headquarters, where Mori's body lay in state. Major Koga kneeled at the foot of General Mori's coffin, put a pistol to his chest, and pulled the trigger. The news was telephoned to his father-in-law, who told his daughter about it. She was quite prepared, having expected it for some time.

The two men distributing their handbills in front of the Palace stopped and disappeared into the pine trees near the Nijubashi Gate. Colonel Shiizaki did what he felt he had to do, in the ceremonial fashion. He turned toward the Palace, took out a dagger, plunged it into his entrails, twisted it, and toppled to the ground. Major Hatanaka stood close to Shiizaki and, using the pistol with which he may have shot General Mori, shot himself through the head.

Adm. Takijiro Onishi, whose high point had come when he had devised the Kamikaze method of attack, knew that his day was over. His attempts to stall the surrender by use of mass Kamikaze attacks on the invaders had been rejected out of hand. He had gone to his official residence and there killed himself in the traditional fashion. An outspoken, arrogant man, he would have had trouble living with the conquerors, even if his code had not made it necessary for him to atone for his sin—failure.

Navy Capt. Yasuna Kozono, the die-hard commander of the Atsugi Naval Air Base, was having difficulties with everyone, as well as with his malaria. The day before the speech, he had visited Admiral Kudo in Yomosuka to forestall trouble from a different naval faction. Kozono had explained that his enemy was the United States; he wanted to fight the Americans, not his countrymen. Admiral Kudo heard him out and tried to soothe him. The next day, after hearing the Emperor's rescript, Kozono gave a pep talk to the officers and men at the base, promising them a national war, the defense of the country by each individual.

The men at Atsugi were busy, and they kept the printing press at the base busy too. Soon leaflets began fluttering down on Tokyo, reading: "Government and senior statesmen who were caught in an enemy trap have enticed the Emperor to issue the message ending the war. It was a terrible thing to do. The Emperor is a God. There is no such thing as surrender in Japan. There is no surrender in the Imperial forces. We, as members of the Air Force, are sure of victory."

This got, for Kozono, a visit from his superior, Admiral Teraoka. During a discussion, the admiral asked Kozono for an explanation of his disobedience. Kozono presented the standard reasons and then added a new one, that the Emperor's declaration of the end of the war showed his mind was afflicted. Teraoka left after warning Kozono to be careful. He reported Kozono's remarks to Admiral Yonai, who asked Prince Takamatsu, the Emperor's brother and a friend of Kozono's, to convince Kozono to forget his mad schemes. The Prince phoned the air base, but Kozono wouldn't listen to him.

Yonai sent some men to talk to Kozono the next day, but a normal conversation was no longer possible. Late the night before, Kozono's problems and frustrations had become too much for him; his mind had snapped. He was put in a strait jacket and then institutionalized.

Gen. Seiichi Tanaka, the man finally responsible for breaking up the officers' plot, brooded for several days. There was never any question about his loyalty to the Emperor. But as head of the Eastern District Army, it was his job to protect Tokyo, and that included, of course, the Emperor. He had had to watch helplessly as selected areas of Tokyo were flattened, raid by raid, by American planes. When a portion of the Palace was destroyed, late in May, he felt as though he had completely failed. The young officers' coup attempt on the night and morning of August 14 and 15 was the last straw.

Despite the fact that no one, least of all the Emperor, questioned his loyalty and devotion to duty, Tanaka was convinced that he was, in some way, responsible for the Japanese defeat, that he had disgraced the Emperor. He could not bear the idea of being the military man in charge of the Tokyo area when the conquering Americans came. Before that, Seiichi Tanaka, a resolute officer, educated at Oxford, went to his office, put on his full-dress uniform, sat down at his desk, and shot himself.

A group of soldiers, unhappy at the idea of surrender, had moved into the Ueno Park area of Tokyo from Mito, about sixty miles north, with ideas of staging a coup of their own. The *Kempeitai,* not wanting to let this develop into an incident, decided to use one of their prisoners, Maj. Sadakichi Ishihara, who had been working with Koga and Hatanaka earlier and had been turned over to the Army police. Ishihara was supposed to be a friend of the leader of the group camped at Ueno Park, so he was released by the *Kempeitai* to try to talk the rebellious group into disbanding and going home.

Ishihara went to the park and asked for his friend. A soldier asked him who he wanted and shot him dead. The man he'd come to see was called; at his expression, his aide took out his sword and killed Ishihara's killer. The leader of the group had enough. When he was asked to disband his group, he did so.

After the Emperor's speech, Captain Sasaki's student soldiers tried to give themselves up at an Army police headquarters that was in itself a shambles. The men were told to turn themselves in to the Tokyo police and did so. They were held there, and later tried. Five of them received five-year sentences, which were later reduced to a year and a half.

Captain Sasaki, however, went into hiding, and stayed

under cover for the fourteen-year period of proscription. In 1959, after he could no longer legally be charged, he reportedly went to see Hajime Suzuki, the premier's son and aide, and apologized. Hajime Suzuki tried to comfort him.

Captain Uehara, of the Air Force Academy, the man who is presumed to have killed General Mori's brother-in-law, Colonel Shiraishi, continued to try to stir up resistance after the Emperor's speech and failed. He, too, killed himself.

Unless a man leaves a document or has a discussion on the subject, it is usually difficult to determine what motivates a man to kill himself. In the cases of the Japanese after the middle of August, 1945, the suicides can be divided into two general types, one being the persons, military or civilian, who felt a deep national shame and wanted to do the right thing, for themselves and their families and the other being the ones who had been involved in the unsuccessful coup d'état.

Some of those, smaller fry, had guilts of a different kind. The soldier who had punched and knocked down Chamberlain Tokugawa came to see him fifteen years later. He apologized for the action and brought a small gift, a family heirloom.

Some of the suicide attempts were sincerely made, but failed. General Tojo, former Premier who had led his country into the disastrous war, waited until his name appeared on a wanted list, September 11, before he shot himself in the chest. After several hours, he was saved by American doctors so he could be tried and killed legally.

Another top general was more successful in his attempt. Field Marshal Gen (Gen is his first name, not an abbreviation of rank) Sugiyama, who had been War Minister in Koiso's cabinet and a long-time conservative officer, did away with himself on September 12. He was not able to do this earlier because he had been entrusted with a delicate task, to move the Japanese troops in the Tokyo area out of the way of the American occupation forces as they took over the capital region. The day after all the Japanese troops been moved north of the Mito River, he followed Tojo's example. Field Marshal Sugiyama went into his office, sat down at his desk, and fired a service revolver into his heart. Unlike Tojo, he died almost instantly.

Another high-ranking suicide was Prince Fumimaro Konoye, a member of the Imperial family, a man of intelligence and, in general, good will, whose peace efforts had been spectacularly ineffectual. Like many upper-class Japanese, he was afraid of what the reactionary civil and military people would do, in addition to which he had an almost pathological fear that the left would coalesce under Communist leadership and completely change Japan politically and socially.

When he learned that he would be arraigned as a war criminal, Prince Konoye took poison. He left a note which stated: "I have made many political blunders since the China Incident, for which I feel deep responsibility, but it is unbearable to me to be tried in an American court as a so-called war criminal. . . ." He also left by his deathbed a copy of Oscar Wilde's *De Profundis,* with an underlined paragraph which began: "I must say to myself that I ruined myself, and that nobody, great or small, can be ruined except by his own hand."

The Emperor was very upset by Konoye's suicide. The brilliant, worldly wise prince was a man Hirohito had trusted and admired, despite his diplomatic failures, which were not always his fault. He had never expected the prince to die in such an undistinguished manner. The Japanese people, in general, still admired seppuku under certain circumstances. They looked down on the use of poison for the purpose; it was an unmanly way out. Konoye obviously felt that he had let down both the people of Japan and the Emperor by his repeated failures, which included not only his inability to keep his homeland out of what he could see would be a disastrous war, but his inability to extricate her at the end. As a proud man he preferred killing himself to standing trial. However, that still did not explain why a man of royal blood would use poison.

Poison was accepted by the Japanese people as a means for a woman to commit suicide; after all, she was not expected to be physically strong enough to use a sword or dagger to take her own life. Japanese women, of course, for centuries have been doing other tasks that take great physical strength—but these were more likely to be peasant women, and ritual self-sacrifice was a luxury of the upper classes. Not only was the old Japan a male-oriented society, it had only recently been changed from a feudal society. The use of a firearm instead of the traditional sword or dagger had only lately become an acceptable method of self-destruction for men. So, while Prince Konoye was criticized for his use of poison, General Tojo was not criticized for using a revolver, but only for bungling the attempt. General Sugiyama was not condemned for the use of a revolver, nor was Mrs. Sugiyama for poisoning herself after she received the expected news of her husband's act.

Things were changing rapidly all over Japan. They had to; the country was in an appalling state, which became even more evident once the war ended and the people did not have the bond of a common enemy and effort to hold themselves together. All they had during the early days at the end of the war was fear. In this case it was the exaggerated fear of a long-isolated and xenophobic people of a strange people with a completely different culture of whom they had heard many strange and frightening tales—some of which had undoubtedly been put out by the Army to frighten the people so that they would support their "fight on at any cost" policy.

Almost immediately after the Emperor's rescript was

broadcast, Premier Suzuki and his whole cabinet handed in their resignations. His had been a caretaker cabinet, a temporary group of respected citizens whose job was to end the war on the best possible terms for Japan. And although Suzuki slowed the action at times by issuing some bellicose statements that alarmed the more moderate Japanese, in general he had done his job. Probably his most remarkable activity was his activity—his ability to keep going, to keep his mind clear, during the hectic period before the broadcast of August 15.

Kantaro Suzuki had been an old man at the time he took office, he was extremely hard of hearing, smoked too many cigars, drank five cups of sake a day, appeared senile, and was obviously too old and weak, some thought, to have such a crucial job entrusted to him. But during the last few days of the war, he seemed able to keep going as long as necessary. The regrets he expressed to the Emperor on resigning were primarily for having had to call on His Majesty, not once but twice, to intervene.

On Suzuki's resignation, the Emperor asked Marquis Kido to recommend a successor. Kido asked for permission to talk this over with Baron Hiranuma, head of the Privy Council. The two men discussed the possibilities, and decided upon Prince Naruhiko Higashi-kuni, on the theory that a member of the royal family would have the best chance of getting the country's support in the difficult days ahead.

The Higashi-kuni cabinet had almost all new ministers, many of them having been second or third men in their departments. Only one of the previous ministers was renamed to his post; Mitsumasa Yonai remained as Minister of the Navy. Mamoru Shigemitsu became Minister for Foreign Affairs; Iwao Yamazaki, the Minister for Home Affairs; Juichi Tsushima, the Minister of Finance; Sadamu Shimomura, the Minister of War; and Chuzo Iwata, the Minister of Justice; other new men were also brought in to administer the country under the guidance of the new rulers.

There were many troubles and problems during that odd period when there was no shooting war but there was no official peace. American and other Allied prisoners of war had to be freed and given food and medical treatment, something that could not always be done tactfully. After American, British, and Dutch prisoners of war who needed aid were taken care of, food had to be brought in for the Japanese, whose diet had dropped to a minimum level.

American troops were coming in to take over the country. The first major contingent would be landing at, of all places, Atsugi, that stronghold of the die-hard Naval air arm. To get things in order, and to greet the conqueror, Atsugi had been put under the command of Lt. Gen. Seizu Arisue, the Imperial Army's Intelligence head. General Arisue found the big air base a mess. It had been badly damaged by American bombings, and to the normal war damage had been added the damage caused by a small civil war.

To keep the die-hards at Atsugi from using their aircraft to do anything rash, the government had sent Army units to the Naval air base to dismantle and remove enough engine parts so that the planes could not be used for any last-ditch heroics. Had the men stationed there been ordered to do it, they would have refused. To have outsiders, Army outsiders, doing it provoked a small shooting war. Both sides were made up of bitter, frustrated, disappointed men. What started as an occasional squabble became a destructive battle, Japanese against Japanese. In due time, the superior numbers of the visitors won out, the planes were rendered inoperable, and the Kamikaze pilots were moved out.

On August 28, the vanguard of the occupation troops landed at Atsugi, having flown in from Okinawa. Despite fears on both sides, there were no untoward incidents. The following day, elements of an airborne division started landing, and the occupation was on in earnest. Early in the afternoon, Gen. Douglas MacArthur landed at Atsugi and proceeded by motorcade to nearby Yokohama and eventually, Tokyo.

Between August 15 and the official signing of the surrender documents on the battleship *Missouri* on September 2, 1945, the Emperor issued two rescripts to the armed forces, one on August 17, the other on August 22, instructing them to lay down their arms and obey the cease-fire. To make sure these orders were received and heeded, the Emperor sent members of his family to key headquarters, such as those of the Kwantung Army, the China Area Fleet, and the China Expeditionary Force.

On September 2, aboard the battleship *Missouri*, in Tokyo Bay, the Articles of Surrender were signed by Shigemitzu for the Foreign Office, Umezu for Imperial General Headquarters, and Douglas MacArthur as Supreme Commander for the Allied Powers.

Once again the Emperor of Japan was a spiritual rather than a temporal ruler. He could get out of the limelight where he wasn't comfortable, and the country could be run by a new shogunate. This time it was an American group, headed by MacArthur. General MacArthur had had his admirers and detractors, both before and after he became the Proconsul in Japan, but few deny that acting as the ruler of Japan, he did an outstanding job.

MacArthur might have been made for the job. The Japanese at the time seemed to want and need an authority figure, and that he was. Conquering occupation troops and their regimes are rarely popular with the inhabitants of the invaded country, and there were many points of friction between the Japanese and Americans. But the immediate postwar occupation of Japan has to be viewed as one of the most successful in history, and a certain amount of that success must be credited to MacArthur's effect on the Japanese. He may have been, as his detractors said, stubborn, egotistical, and overly dramatic, but he had the panache the people seemed to want and need at the time.

CHAPTER XI

Some Questions
and Conclusions

More than a quarter of a century has passed, and many of the people prominent at the time have died of causes ranging from the deterioration of old age to the deterioration caused by radiation.

Many survivors of the bombing of Hiroshima and Nagasaki died in the following weeks and months from radiation. Many of those still living bear visible and invisible scars of the bombing. Some, unmarked physically, cannot get married or find jobs, as it is feared that they carry "the bomb disease." Many children of the area, not yet born in the summer of 1945, have difficulty finding "normal" husbands and wives because of fear of possible genetic damage.

Some of the fears are very real; some are new old wives' tales. It was thought at first, for instance, that Hiroshima and Nagasaki would be uninhabitable for years in the ground zero area. This turned out to be untrue. But studies are still going on in an attempt to assess the genetic effects of atomic radiation, studies whose ultimate conclusions cannot be known until several generations have been born and observed. Yet it no longer seems likely that the horrible effects feared at first will come to pass. What actually happened at the time was horrible enough, of course, even if there are no aftereffects whatever.

The two bombed cities recovered in completely different ways. Hiroshima is still a scarred city, despite rebuilding. No one can forget that it was the first target of the most destructive weapon ever used on earth. Nagasaki, which was a smaller community and not as badly damaged because of its topography, has gone ahead with less looking back.

There are few official reminders of the atomic bomb in Nagasaki. One, at about the center of the ground zero area, is a building called the Nagasaki Cultural Center. It is a modern stone and concrete building that contains objects that survived the atomic blast in changed form—a piece of basalt, for instance, with odd blisters caused by the stone's bubbling from the intense heat of the bomb, a human hand and a large piece of glass fused into a single shape, and other items that were weirdly affected by the intense heat and pressure.

Nearby is the huge Peace Statue, a thirty-two-foot bronze male figure, with one hand lifted to the sky, the other outstretched horizontally. The Cultural Center and Peace Statue are visited by hundreds of thousands annually, including school children from all over Japan. Not too far from the epicenter is the new Urikami Cathedral, which was built to replace Japan's largest Catholic cathedral, completely destroyed by the bomb. The new cathedral can be seen from Glover House, not destroyed, supposedly the place where Cho-cho-san in Puccini's *Madame Butterfly* awaited the return of her American lover, Lieutenant Pinkerton.

In the old portion of the town is a low concrete building that houses a joint American–Japanese investigative group, the Atomic Bomb Casualty Commission, whose purpose is to keep track of survivors of the two atomic blasts. One of the things the commission tries to do is assign the exact reason for Japanese casualties. To this day in Japan, there is a tendency to blame on the atomic bomb every cancer death in the area, every reported case of leukemia, every miscarriage, every malformed child.

That, of course, is true not only in Japan. In April, 1967, when Bob Shumard, one of the crew of the *Enola Gay*, died in Detroit of leukemia after a brief illness, there was speculation about his death being connected with radiation from the Hiroshima bomb. There was no reason to believe that radioactive particles received twenty-two years earlier could set up a condition that would remain latent for that length of time and suddenly become fatal. But if this type of speculation could arise in the United States in 1967, it is easy to imagine how such incidents could be exaggerated in Japan, and particularly the Japan of the decade or two following the end of the war.

There was a question about the possibility of sterilization due to receiving even a small amount of radiation. But Major Sweeney, who flew the instrument plane at the Hiroshima bombing and the strike plane at Nagasaki, is the father of eleven children.

In the last weeks of the war, much depended on chance, much turned on apparent trivialities. We have already seen how critical was the Japanese use of the word *mokusatsu* in their reaction to the Allied declaration at Potsdam. In a sense, the ambiguities inherent in this term may be said to have sealed the fates of Hiroshima and Nagasaki.

An American who spent several years working for the government in Japan after the war has told me that postwar Japan and Far Eastern development might have been quite different if *Bock's Car* had been able to bomb Kokura instead of Nagasaki because Kokura's heavy industry was so useful in rebuilding Japan. I am not convinced it would have made much difference; the heavy industry destroyed in Nagasaki and elsewhere was eventually rebuilt. If Kokura had been bombed as Hiroshima was, the recovery timetable might have been somewhat different, but eventual results probably would have been the same. Incidentally, although Kokura was not bombed, it cannot be found on a modern map of Japan. In 1963, it was incorporated into the city of Kita Kyushu and disappeared as a name and entity.

The debate over the status of the Emperor seems another case in which confusion and mutual misunderstanding, by delaying the end of a war whose issue had been determined, bore awful fruit. What if the United States government had listened to the advice of some of its Japan experts, people such as former Ambassador to Japan Joseph C. Grew, and had made immediate statements that the position of the Emperor would be honored? There are those who think that if we had reached such a conclusion and had made it unmistakably clear, the war would have been ended much sooner. I am not sure.

The undefined status of the Imperial family and particularly of the Emperor gave the die-hards among the militarists a rallying cry and an excuse for objecting to surrender. Had this issue been resolved, most of them would have remained intransigent. They would have switched to another point of contention and another rallying cry. Even when the Emperor said he wanted to accept the Allied terms, that this was his express wish, the militarists found reasons to oppose him—for his own good, of course.

The arguments about the status of the Emperor were as bitter in Washington, London, and Moscow as they were in Japan. Washington was carrying the ball for the Allies in the negotiations to end the war. Former Ambassador Grew, as noted, led the fight to retain the Emperor, at least as the nominal head of the government. Others in the Department of State, including former Secretary Hull, could see no reason for our democratic government to condone the continuation by a beaten enemy of the institution of royalty. Some Depart-

ment of State leaders advised making concessions so that the
Emperor would remain, simply because they were anxious to
do anything to end the war quickly.

There were a lot of arguments against concession, some of
them making domestic political sense, others caused by fear
of loss of face. Just as the Japanese military commanders
could not see how they could accede to the surrender demands
after having announced so many victories, so some American
military and political leaders would find it difficult to eat
the words they or their public relations spokesmen had so
recklessly spouted describing the things they would do to the
Japanese Emperor. Both sides paid the penalty for believing
some of their own propaganda. How could an American
politician agree to the retention of the Emperor without
worry about being accused of appeasement by current or
future opponents?

On the American side, much of the argument about the
treatment and status of the Emperor was theoretical. It
seemed a minor point. We had won a complete victory, and
our conditions included unconditional surrender. How could
there be any bargaining over terms? On the other hand, many
of the same people that were worrying about Japan's delay
in accepting these terms were aware that every day that
passed after August 9, the Russian armies were taking control
of more of Manchuria. There had already been postwar
difficulties with the Soviet Union about Berlin and Germany
and the governments of eastern European countries; we
didn't want the pattern repeated in the Orient.

Oddly enough, more opposition to the Japanese retention
of the Emperor came from monarchical Britain than repub-
lican America. China didn't seem to care much; she just
wanted to get the Japanese out. The Russians seemed more
interested in establishing Soviet hegemony in areas adjoining
her homeland than in determining whether or not Japan
was to be under Imperial rule. And while the role of the

Emperor seemed a theoretical question to the Allies, it was intensely practical to the Japanese because it was an essential part of their whole way of life. Fortunately, the more moderate faction won in America. The Emperor was not put in a cage and exhibited to the world, nor did Admiral Halsey ride the Emperor's white horse through the streets of Tokyo. And fortunately, the Japanese Foreign Minister was the moderate Togo, and the War Minister was the comparatively reasonable Anami, whose loyalty to his country and Emperor would not allow him to resign and thus precipitate a government crisis.

Those Allied policymakers who said it was necessary for the Emperor to remain, thereby giving the Japanese government a core, a center through which surrender terms could be administered, turned out to be correct. The confusion was great enough as it was.

One of the reasons that some Americans favored the retention of the Emperor, as we have mentioned, was a desire to hurry along the surrender process and to keep some sort of orderly government in power, rather than enter into a period of confusion that might end with Japanese Communists in power. This was also a reason some of the Japanese accepted what seemed to them harsh terms. The Japanese ruling class seemed to have the same, almost paranoiac fear of Russia and communism (with more cause, if for no other reason than geography) that a certain type of American showed in the 1950s.

In some respects, no two military partners could have been farther apart in outlook and customs than the Japanese and Germans of the early 1940s. In other ways, they were markedly similar. The Japanese governmental system was comparatively old and established, having followed more or less the same pattern since before the turn of the century; in Germany the Nazis were new, having been in power only a few years. The ruling politicians of both countries had a notable, and by their lights reasonable, fear of letting the people decide major issues for themselves on the basis of any free exchange of information; both governments had entered openly upon a campaign of conquest, using as a reason the need for raw materials, expansion, and the stifling, encircling tactics of their enemies.

By tradition and training, the people of both countries had a respect for authority, uniform, and government. However, while the Japanese militarists had, for some time, run the government, in Germany the militarists *were* the government. The Nazi leader was Hitler, who made the important decisions. The Japanese Emperor, as we have seen, normally made no decisions, certainly not military ones. Officially, until he dropped the idea in 1946, he was the descendant of the Sun Goddess; officially he was the nation's spiritual ruler, a responsibility he took seriously, even if he could not believe in the myth of his descent.

After the war ended disastrously for them, both the German and Japanese people and some of their leaders proclaimed to the world and their conquerors that they had been part of the peace-loving faction all along. Some, of course, were not able to do that; they were too totally on the record. It was not easy to sort out the sincere leaders who fought against the war, particularly in Japan, because many of them had changed course, not necessarily as opportunists.

Baron Hiranuma, for instance, had been for many years a rightist, a supernationalist. He had been one of the men responsible for the overthrow of the reform-minded Wakatsuki cabinet in 1927, and had helped install a right-wing general as Premier. When he was made Premier in 1939, he became less reactionary as he came to realize the power the Army possessed. He turned against the unbridled expansion of the Kwantung Army; by 1941, he was so out of favor with the fanatics that he was the target of an assassination attempt. He opposed the war with the United States, not so much because he was antiwar, but because he didn't think Japan could win. When Tojo came to power, Hiranuma was dropped. As head of the Privy Council, a purely advisory body, he was present at Inner Council meetings, although he had no legal right to be there. And although he worked hard to get the council members to see that the only thing to do was to accept the Emperor's point of view and the Potsdam proclamation, by August 12 he had turned around again and was supporting Anami's "protect the Emperor" campaign.

Prince Konoye, though he did not achieve any of his objectives, seems to have been a sincerely peaceful man. His rank was enough to protect him from dangers that might have come to others. It was not only that he was against the war with the United States, he was against war, although he was so afraid of the threat of communism that he might have approved of a war against the Soviet Union.

Admiral Yonai, former premier and out of the government because of his antiwar bias for some time after 1940, was not as outspoken as Prince Konoye in earlier days. However, like Togo and Suzuki, he had memories of assassination attempts. In the late 1930s, Admiral Yonai had spent a good deal of time and effort successfully blocking the Army's attempt to work out a pact with Germany. The only agreement with Germany to which he would have agreed would have been one devoted solely to fighting the Soviet Union.

The Nazi–Soviet nonaggression pact of 1939 for a time changed the Japanese picture so completely that the government then in power fell. Yonai, with a somewhat pro-American and pro-British attitude, headed the new government despite the vociferous opposition of the Army. However, when the war broke out in Europe and the Nazi Army was sweeping all before it, he was forced to resign. The Army wanted to conclude an alliance with Germany while Hitler was still in the mood to listen to them. But by the end of November, 1941, just a few days before Pearl Harbor, Admiral Yonai seemed to have joined the prowar forces.

At that time, the military had succeeded in placing a time limit on the negotiations going on in Washington, planning soon to begin its attacks on outposts of the United States, Britain, and the Netherlands. The Emperor, who was trying to guide Premier Konoye into putting off the deadline, had been consulting with the cabinet and elder statesmen, the *jushin*. Two of the former premiers who knew the situation fairly well expressed their doubts about Japan's material capacity to wage the type of war outlined. Prince Konoye, on being asked, answered with regret that further negotiations seemed hopeless, but still asked whether it might not be possible to find a way out of the current deadlock by persevering. Admiral Yonai, however, seemed to adopt the militarists' policy. He quoted an old saying that by trying to avoid going broke in the future, Japan was in danger of going bankrupt now.

Another former premier spoke against starting a war for the purpose of establishing the Greater East Asia Co-Prosperity Sphere or for other purposes not directly connected with self-defense. But Premier Tojo spoke up strongly, forecasting that military plans which had been made would give Japan strategic points in the Pacific that would enable her to fight a long war. He carried the day.

While we, in far-off America, generally regarded the Japanese state as similar to the German government under Hitler, the Italian government under Mussolini, or the Russians under Stalin, as a monolithic structure under the Emperor, there were strains and differences of opinion in Japan we did not realize. We knew the Emperor was venerated; we did not realize he was, in some practical respects, a figurehead. He was not expected to be a policymaker; he was expected to give his approval to policies already decided upon by the men who ran the various departments. If he had a point of view on a particular matter, he had to work subtly, through a man like Marquis Kido, his contact with government officials.

It was seemingly a complicated system, and one depending on a certain amount of trust and insight. How was a minister to know whether Kido was passing on word from the Emperor or giving his own opinion, or perhaps had been influenced by someone else? The Japanese had a reputation of being subtle, socially, and they carried this through to their politics. In their political dealings, they often used the technique of *haragei*, the device of saying one thing but meaning another.

An example of the problems of indirect attack had come in Tokyo in 1941 at the September 6 Imperial conference. The Emperor told Kido before the conference started that he would not sanction war as long as there was a chance of peace. Kido, anticipating such an attitude from his previous remarks, had already briefed someone to ask the proper questions. Statements were made, the questions asked, and after a fashion, answered. Lip service was being given to the subject of continuing the diplomatic discussions, while it was taken for granted that they would be futile and war plans would go on.

At this point, the Emperor got up to speak. To everyone's surprise, he did not simply endorse the past speakers. He asked why the War and Navy Ministers had not answered the question as to which should have priority, war or diplomatic talks? He said that as far as he was concerned, he had no doubt of the answer and then read a poem written by his grandfather, the Emperor Meiji: "The seas surround all quarters of the globe/ And my heart cries out to the nations of the world/ Why then do the winds and waves of strife/ Disrupt the peace between us?" (*"Yomono umi/ Miniharakarato Omouyoni/ Nado Adamino/ Tachisawaguran?"*)

The men at the meeting got the general idea: the Emperor

would prefer peace. He thought he had done a good deal; he had expressed his wishes. There was no doubt they were understood.

But he had not ordered the plans to be changed.

All that happened as a result was that the time for the Japanese offensive move was postponed. It was suggested through Ambassador Grew that a meeting between Prince Konoye and President Roosevelt be set up to work out a way to avoid what seemed to be an inevitable war. There was never any answer to Grew's plea for these talks. Later it was revealed that the American Department of State was of the opinion that talks with Japanese envoys were unimportant, that no matter what the diplomats said, the Japanese military machine was going to move in its own way, doing what it wanted to do. And in truth, the Army and Navy had decided to move, as we know, on December 7. They felt it had to be done now; the joint British–American–Dutch boycott was strangling the Japanese war machine. Its oil reserves were being depleted, and if she couldn't get oil by negotiation, she would get it by direct action, taking over the Far Eastern refineries and oil stocks of others.

The question is raised: If the Emperor of Japan was truly a man of peace, if he was able in 1945, with a good deal of difficulty, to speak up and get his country out of war, why couldn't he have spoken up earlier and kept his country out?

Like most basic questions, this does not have a simple, single answer. Part of the answer lies in the character of the man himself, part in the institution he represented or personified. Americans, who have a tendency to be informal and to personalize institutions, usually referred to him as Hirohito. The Japanese customarily referred to him more respectfully as the Emperor.

This small, shy, and rather introspective man probably gave little thought to the fact that he was the Emperor—

that is what he was born to be and there was no way to change it. He undoubtedly would have been happier had he lived in less troubled times, when he could have spent his time as a ceremonial head of state while the cabinet ran the country with advice from the elder statesmen. He does not have a strong personality, a drive for power, or any great desire to bend people to his way of thinking. Although he was born in the twentieth century—April 29, 1901—he is, in a sense, a traditionalist. This may be one answer to the question of why he didn't speak out strongly against the war before it started. He didn't think it was any of his business; he didn't think it was his right to interfere with his cabinet ministers and advisers. Or perhaps he didn't feel strongly enough about the matter.

That being the case, why did he take a stand to end the war?

That, too, can be looked at in at least two ways. A cynic would say that he didn't speak out openly against the war because he wanted to enjoy the glory of being the head of a conquering nation; that he took a stand in 1945 only because he knew the jig was up and he wanted to save his own skin as well as what was left of his country.

We are working on the assumption that he is not and was not a warlike person, that he sincerely preferred peace. We also have to realize that since he was only forty years old when Japan went to war with the Western powers, he was not too sure of himself or his powers, despite his having been brought up to be Emperor. For a long time, Japan's domestic affairs had been run by the shogunate; for a long time Japan had not had any foreign affairs, she had lived in self-imposed isolation. When Japan had ventured into the outside world, militarily she had done extremely well, defeating in turn her two huge neighbors, China and Russia. In World War I, Japan entered the war on the side of the Allies on August 23, 1914, ostensibly because she was bound to Britain by treaty, but probably also because she was influenced by a desire to get some of the German Pacific territories.

Japanese military adventures had turned out happily for her, but those were in days before Hirohito was the Emperor. In the 1930s, the military took the bit in their teeth and provoked the "China incident" that brought them control of a huge territory. The Emperor reportedly was not pleased, but it was done, a *fait accompli*. Buttressed by a string of victories, all of which seemed unlikely at the beginning, the military set out for big game: Pearl Harbor, Singapore, control of the Pacific.

If the Emperor had really appreciated his power, and if he had really wanted to stop this aggression, he might have been able to do so. But it needed both the knowledge of the use of power and the desire to use it. Leaving out other factors, the Emperor was probably the only man in Japan who could fight the military without real fear. But he didn't do it, and he didn't speak out against this rash adventure. We will probably never know why. But by 1945, it was a different story.

By 1945, the Emperor had become disillusioned with the military. He could point to the "China incident," which was supposed to have been a brief episode but went on for years, to the various campaigns that after 1942 promised victory and ended in defeat, and even to the defenses of the home islands, defenses that either were not built or were far behind schedule. He did not doubt the good will of the military leaders who were making the promises, but he no longer had faith in their capacity to deliver. That was the reason he pinned his faith, mistakenly, on attempts to persuade the Soviet Union to act as an honest broker to end the war.

By the time it got down to direct negotiations, the Emperor knew he had to take a stand. No one else swung enough weight to be effective, and for the preservation of the nation, it was necessary to see that hostilities were halted. The situation was different from the conditions in the weeks before Pearl Harbor. At that time, though the top military men knew the plans, the others in the cabinet did not; they were told only that there were plans and to leave it to the Army and Navy. Even the Foreign Office was kept in the dark as long as possible because the military rightly feared that the Foreign Office people would insist that they live up to previous agreements to give the enemy some warning. While theoretically obeying the letter of the law, the military delivered the warning message too late, as planned, to make any difference.

While the various nonmilitary cabinet ministers had no access to the military's plans, there is no doubt that the Emperor knew them. By August, 1945, the question was not only a matter of survival, but also a divided cabinet. That, of course, was the excuse that Suzuki used to get the Emperor to break tradition and speak. It also made it easier on the Emperor's sense of fitness and tradition. With the groups unable to reach an agreement, he had an excuse to talk to them directly using the unparalleled prestige of his position. Even then, as we know, though he spoke out quite directly, saying what he wanted done, his wishes were not obeyed.

What would have happened had he spoken out so directly prior to December 7, 1941? Probably nothing. Without directly opposing him, the militarists would have worked out a way to go around him. Like the rebellious young officers in August, 1945, they would have been doing it in the Emperor's name and for his own good. What if he had spoken out as strongly for an end to the war at an earlier time, when some of the more practical military leaders knew the Japanese position was going to deteriorate? The chances are he would have ended up with a divided country—all loyal to him, of course, but two camps warring between themselves.

By August, 1945, even the most optimistic military people knew there was no hope of victory. What they were holding out for was the glory of going down in a tragic defeat, of dying in the Samurai tradition. Their rationalization was that the status of the Emperor had not been guaranteed, and that by standing up and fighting to the last man, so to speak, they could inflict such heavy losses that the Allied terms would be eased. It is one of those arguments that make a better sound than they do logic. But if the militarists had been strictly logical, they wouldn't have done many of the things they did, and did successfully for a time. A large number of Kamikaze fighters, whether diving explosive planes or crashing torpedo boats or submarines into enemy craft or fighting on the ground as fearless, because doomed, soldiers, could have inflicted heavy losses on an invading Army, probably not enough to have changed the outcome of the war, but enough to have caused trouble.

The difficulty was that the Japanese were up against an enemy that was too well equipped, that by that time had too many men and machines to be stopped. What the Japanese had to put against this was their vaunted spirit and self-sacrifice, the kind of thing that made for Kamikazes and banzai charges. In this respect, the Japanese are, as all nations seem to be, racists. They believe they are better than other peoples in certain specific qualities. This belief seems to appear in all cultures. For years, the British ruled much of the world with a small Army, a large Navy, and the feeling that they were morally right and that because they'd had the sense or good fortune to be born British, it was their duty to run things. The French, Italians, Germans, Russians, Spaniards all feel much the same way, as do the Chinese, Japanese, Koreans, and others.

The point of this is that each nation is able to look upon the world as being made up of inferiors because the others are white, brown, red, black, or tan; are Protestants, Catholics, Jews, Moslems, Hindus, or Sikhs. The enemy is an alien: He speaks a different tongue, has a different religion, has different customs, and therefore does not have to be treated as an equal, as a man, but as some foreigner, something that can be referred to by a derogatory name—a limey or a Kraut, a Russki, Chink, gook, Yankee, gringo, depending on who's saying what about whom—and thus killed without a qualm. This seemingly universal trait shows up in language in various forms. The word *zulu*, in Zulu, means "man." The word *navajo*, in the Athapascan tongue, means "nation."

This feeling of superiority over others can, in wartime, be both a good and a bad thing. It enables a normally humane man to engage without guilt in that most inhuman activity, warfare, and to kill or mistreat prisoners and civilians. It also enabled the British to continue fighting the Nazis long after they should have known they were beaten, and then to go on and win. It also enabled the Japanese to continue to fight long after they should have known they were beaten, which prolonged the war, meaning more death and casualties, and brought atomic bombs to two cities.

This Japanese sense of being a superior culture was intensified by its background and long period of isolation. Until Matthew Perry and the United States Navy opened it to Western trade in 1854, it had spent much of its history and the past two hundred fifty years in isolation. Earlier, Japan had been strongly influenced, first by Korea and then in the sixth to eighth centuries, by China, when Buddhism was introduced. Primarily feudal in nature, the country spent many centuries waging local civil wars. In 1274 and 1284, the Mongols under Kublai Khan tried to invade the islands, and failed. One failure was due to a violent storm which wrecked their invasion fleet—not unlike what happened to the Spanish Armada. That storm in Japan is known as the Kamikaze, or divine wind, a name borrowed by Onishi and his friends for their suicide fighters.

The first contact with Europe seems to have come in 1542, being brought about by Portuguese sailors. They were followed by the introduction of Christianity in 1549 by Saint Francis Xavier. In the late sixteenth century, three great warriors led the nation. One of them, Hideyoshi, invaded Korea in 1592 and in 1596 in an unsuccessful effort to invade China. This period was followed by two hundred and fifty years of the Iyeyasu family shogunate, which set up a central government that was efficient but repressive. Christianity was suppressed, and all intercourse with foreign countries prohibited, except with the Dutch who were allowed to have a single trading post which was located in Nagasaki. Although Perry's ships changed the course of Japan, the isolation era officially ended in 1868 with the so-called Meiji Restoration, putting power back into the hands of the royal family. In 1889, Japan became a constitutional government, using a constitution based on that of Prussia. In 1894, Japan went to war with a weakened, divided China, and took Formosa and the Pescadores, as well as the Liaotung peninsula in Manchuria, which the Big Powers forced her to return. In 1904, Japan went to war with Russia, and though Theodore Roosevelt imposed a peace treaty at Portsmouth, the action raised Japan to the status of a major power. In 1910, she annexed Korea.

All this had its effect on the twentieth-century Japanese warriors. They may not have known the long history of Japanese attempts to dominate China when, in 1931, they created the incidents in Mukden that gave them an opportunity to take over Manchuria, but they were following a precedent. And as a tradition-conscious people, the Japanese followed other precedents in her dealings. Her basic fear of Russia and communism has been based on the proximity of a powerful neighbor, and more. The 1904-1905 war and victory gave Japan a shot in the arm. After the end of World War I, when Allied troops went to Russia and stayed in Siberia for a number of reasons, the Japanese kept troops there longer than any other nation.

The long period of previous isolation made it difficult for the Japanese to adjust to outsiders. It also bred its own form of standards and values. The family came first, friends and townspeople next, other Japanese followed; there was very little place for consideration of others, of aliens, which in a way explains some of the seeming contradictions that have bothered many observers.

Americans visiting in postwar Japan have come away, as a rule, charmed and tremendously impressed, not just by the Japanese success, but by their sense of design and their politeness. Closer observers have discovered that this politeness is not general. The Japanese, who bumps into a friend just so that he can apologize profusely, will also bump into a stranger without giving it a second thought.

This may answer a question that has puzzled many: Can these charming, polite people be the same ones whose reign in Korea and China and various Pacific islands was notorious for its cruelty and lack of consideration? The answer is yes. Can these polite, punctilious people be the same whose treatment of American war prisoners, for instance, was in many authenticated cases sadistic or murderous? The answer again is yes. Consistency by our standards is not necessarily consistency by theirs. The Japanese have had little more than a hundred years to join the rest of the world. Their society was, and in many ways still is, dictated by rigid codes. These codes do not always take in the problems raised by the twentieth century. There is a Japanese saying, a form of code in itself, that would seem to explain much of the appalling Japanese conduct during the war: "No shame away from home."

The Japanese people have overcome so many obstacles that it is not difficult to see how they might be able to delude themselves into thinking they could take on America, Britain, China, and the rest. Their home islands are not an Eden. A population of one hundred million is crammed together on a land area somewhat smaller than that of Montana, and of Japan's 142,000 square miles, only about 20 percent is arable. This means that most of the people live on coastal and other plains, squeezed together tighter than the Dutch or Belgians. Such population pressure requires a precise code of living with sharply defined limits. It also furnished Japan with the excuse it needed for expansion. Too poor to feed itself, the country needed colonies to supply it with food, raw materials for its industries, and customers for its products.

There is a certain amount of irony in this argument. Since 1945, Japan has been stripped of its colonies, new and old, yet today Japan is much more prosperous and better fed than ever before. With a larger population than before, most of it having moved since the war from the farms to the cities on the coastal areas, Japan is today a rice-exporting nation, no longer dependent on imports for its food staples. Japan, with very limited natural resources, now has a gross national product greater than that of England or Germany, overshadowed only by the two colossi, the United States and Soviet Russia. In retrospect, this makes the old expansionist arguments look foolish, foolish as was the militarists' argument that they could not surrender because there was no word for *surrender* in the soldiers' rule book.

Because of the behavior of its citizens abroad, and because of its success, Japan has become unpopular in much of Asia. The Japanese business traveler is regarded as is the American of Asia. Japanese postwar success has brought to it many of the troubles and problems of America. The rapidly improving standard of living has brought on the desire for more physical comforts, and along with it, traffic jams that make New York and London seem sane and spacious, an air-pollution problem that is horrific, and a youth revolt that seems louder than that in America, though somewhat more formalized. The so-called generation gap seems to be as wide as that in America, but with at least one basic difference—the radical young Japanese, having dinner at home before going out to demonstrate, is apt to make a deep bow to the honorable ancestors before sitting down to eat.

There are contrasts in today's Japan that were present during the war, but are just not as noticeable. A people of independent bent, they are notably wont to be governed by consensus; a people of precise good manners and delicacy, they can show an amazing rudeness, coarseness, and cruelty; a people with a great desire to be liked and admired, they behave at times in a way to put off their most open-minded would-be admirers. There are elements in their national character that probably will never be understood by Americans, by even the most empathetic, and the same is undoubtedly true of their understanding of Americans. All these contradictory traits helped bring on a war that might have been avoided and prolong it after it might have been stopped. Yet the American occupation of Japan was probably the most successful military occupation ever conducted.

During the last few days of the war, even though we didn't know what was taking place in Japan, and wouldn't have understood much of it if we had, we could understand results. Through the Potsdam proclamation, we had, by our lights, given the Japanese an opportunity to surrender and save themselves from further punishment. No satisfactory answer was received about the Potsdam terms until much later. Because the proclamation did not mention atomic bombs, the destruction it hinted at could have been regarded as just more enemy propaganda. On the other hand, if we had detailed the bomb, chances are their government and military people would not have believed us and would have made every effort to keep the news from the people. In addition, we would have lost the psychological value of the bomb.

Which brings us to the question of whether either atomic bomb was necessary, of whether there could not have been another method of showing its power without destroying a large portion of two cities, killing a quarter of a million people in the process? The arguments for and against the use of the nuclear bombs are fairly well known, but they may bear repeating briefly.

Against: The bomb is inhuman, which causes unimaginable future problems, as well as immediate destruction by heat, pressure, and radiation. It wasn't necessary. Japan was well beaten by that time. All we had to do was continue our conventional bombing and, of course, continue the plans for the fall and spring invasions of the islands. The damage we had caused to the Japanese transportation system, as well as to their productive facilities, would be enough to bring them to surrender.

For: The proponents of the use of the atomic bomb say, in effect, that it is no more inhuman, or not significantly more, than conventional bombing. The fire-bombing of Tokyo caused more deaths than the atomic bomb at Nagasaki and destroyed a larger area of the city than either atomic bomb. The fire-bombing of Hamburg and Dresden also caused more casualties and destruction. Outside of radiation, the major difference in the type of bombs used is that the atomic bombs can cause all this destruction with just one bomb instead of hundreds or thousands. Consequently, it makes little difference to someone who is killed, wounded, or has his family, home, business, or city destroyed whether it is caused by a thousand planes dropping a thousand bombs or one plane dropping one bomb. They also maintain that the shock value of the atomic bomb was one of the factors that knocked Japan out of the war; without its use, they contend, more people, both Japanese and Allied, would have been killed by conventional weapons and the bloody work of invasion.

One of the theories current now, but not at the time of its use, is that as a "racist" nation, we would only have used the atomic bomb against a nonwhite people, which is nonsense. For one thing, the decision to build the bomb, and to hurry it, was based primarily on a desire to beat the Nazis to it. It was being rushed, but as time went on, it became obvious that the war in Europe would be over before the bomb would be ready. The most convincing argument against this "racist" theory is that in December, 1944, during the Battle of the Bulge, President Roosevelt called in the Manhattan Project's General Groves to ask whether the atomic bomb couldn't be rushed so that it could be used to stop the desperate Nazi counteroffensive. General Groves had to say no. He wasn't at all sure at the time that they were going to be able to make their target date of August 1, 1945, then seven and a half months away. As a matter of fact, as he admitted much later, despite the confidence he showed, he wasn't at all sure the bomb could be built, or if it were, would be successful.

This was just one of the reasons the military was against the proposal that the bomb be demonstrated on an open place before being dropped on a city. The scientists believed in the bomb; the military, as a whole, didn't—those few who knew about it, that is. For instance, there had been a proposal that the first bomb be detonated in a well-advertised drop over Tokyo Bay so that the Japanese military and government officials and the rest of the populace could see its power. One of the reasons that this proposal was rejected was the fear of failure. Another was the worry that advance advertising would enable the Japanese to set up their defenses and possibly destroy the plane and the bomb before it reached the target area. There was also the fear that a display of such a weapon might not convince the enemy, and then its shock value would be lost, for good.

There was another factor that wasn't realized until a little later. An atomic bomb of the Hiroshima type might look very impressive—it would be, in effect, a monumental bang—but its truly devastating effect wasn't known to us until the Alamogordo test three weeks before Hiroshima, and even that wasn't conclusive. It had been a static test—a stationary bomb suspended from a metal tower—not a weapon being dropped from a plane under wartime conditions. No true indication of the destructive power of the atomic bomb could have been demonstrated to nonscientific observers by a test drop over Tokyo Bay.

This in turn brings up the question of whether it was necessary to use the second bomb, the one at Nagasaki. Actually, it was used even sooner than originally scheduled. When the Hiroshima mission was set for August 6, the second bomb was supposed to be used five days later, on the eleventh. Many members of the crew of the *Enola Gay*, on the way back to Tinian after the bombing of Hiroshima, did not expect the second bomb to be used at all. After seeing what they had seen, they expected that by the time they got back to their base, the war would be over. No government, they felt, could subject its land and its people to such punishment, such devastation.

They did not count on the reaction of the Japanese military, who did not believe the reports, who felt the incident must have been a fluke of some sort, who were not convinced that there was more than one bomb, and who did everything possible to keep the actual news from the people of Japan. The men who flew the Hiroshima mission did not count on the disbelief of even their own friends on Tinian. Flyers who had not witnessed the Hiroshima bombing could not take in its effect. It was, when the *Enola Gay* first returned, just words. After pictures were available, it became more real, but still remained just a record of terrible damage. Those who hadn't been there and hadn't seen it themselves couldn't take in the thought of that much devastation being contained in one package, even a large package.

The Hiroshima mission flyers were a little surprised when the second bomb was rescheduled for the ninth, moved up by two days, because a storm was forming. Otherwise the mission would have had to be put off for possibly a week. So the Los Alamos scientists and technicians who were part of the Tinian task force worked nonstop for a time in their small, well-guarded area assembling the elements that would turn the assorted pieces of metal, wire, and chemicals into a lethal weapon. It was finished in time. *Bock's Car* took off on August 9, beating the predicted storm, with results that are known.

The questions about the results remain. Could they have been achieved without the use of the second bomb, without the estimated seventy-five thousand casualties at Nagasaki?

The conclusion I've reached is that the results could not have been achieved without the use of the second bomb.

America and the Allies would have won the war without the atomic bomb. Japan was thoroughly beaten, though still dangerous, before the bomb was used at Hiroshima and Nagasaki. But whether the war would have been won without more months of bombing and shelling and suffering, culminating in the projected invasion of Kyushu in the fall and of Honshu in the spring is another question.

This is a question that has been argued, usually quite emotionally, for some time. It is a basic reason for my having researched and written this book. I was trying to find out: Was the Nagasaki bomb necessary, or was it used because two bombs had been programmed and no one thought to stop the second one after the success of the first?

Leaving out the question of the morality of using the atomic bomb itself, this book confines itself to the second bomb. The arguments on the morality of any atomic weapon are endless. They can be boiled down to this: It was wartime;

war is a matter of taking human life and is therefore in itself immoral. We developed the atomic bomb and we used it. We had very little doubt that if the Germans or Japanese had developed an atomic bomb first, they would have used it. The question becomes one of degree. Is it that much worse to kill a hundred thousand people with a single bomb than it is to kill one person with a single bullet? Is it worse than killing a hundred thousand people with a thousand bombs, as at Tokyo or Dresden or London, Rotterdam or Coventry?

The atomic bomb is new, appallingly destructive, and kills in a different way from the bombs to which we have become accustomed. It also has a delayed effect. All this, many people, with good reason, consider horrible. But this is not the basic problem. Dr. Albert Einstein, the man whose theories were largely responsible for the successful manufacture of the atomic bomb, was disturbed at the thought that man might not have the social or political competence to be in possession of an atomic weapon, that perhaps it had been built too soon in the evolution of man and society.

However, once it was accepted that there was such a thing as an atomic bomb, that one had been built and used, the question became not whether the use of atomic fission in a bomb was proper, but whether the second bomb served a useful purpose, whether it bore any relationship to the amount of suffering it caused. Because of this, most of the preceding chapters have been about conditions inside Japan during another ten days that shook the world, the period starting at Hiroshima August 6 and ending with the Emperor's rescript of August 15, 1945.

What was going on in Washington, London, and Moscow is fairly well known. So far as Washington and London are concerned, there have been many articles and books by participants and observers telling what was happening, in the way of events, and what was going on in the minds of many of the people who had power over the events. What was going on in Japan at the time was not known at all to Americans and is not well known to Americans today.

The bombing of Nagasaki did not end the war. It did give the Emperor a means by which to convince the military that the Potsdam terms had to be accepted. It gave some of the military a way out—accept surrender because the atomic bomb was not a weapon to which a people, no matter how brave or how full of patriotism, could stand up. In effect, it became a method of saving face for the military. It gave them an excuse to follow the Emperor's wishes to surrender.

The bombs used at Hiroshima and Nagasaki are fire-crackers compared to the many-megaton bombs now in the arsenal of certain powers. If these are ever used, we will deserve what we receive. *We* does not refer to any particular nationality. It refers to us all as human beings.

Hiroshima has a Peace Park, in which is a memorial to those who died from atomic bombing. The inscription on the memorial reads: Rest in peace. The mistake shall not be repeated.

The bomb was used twice in 1945. It is understandable how that could happen at that time, how they were useful. It shouldn't happen again.

Bob Lewis, copilot of the plane that dropped the first bomb on Hiroshima, said many years later:

I feel strongly that if some of the heads of state could have seen what the crew of the Enola Gay saw that day, they'd redouble their efforts to see that the power of the atom is used for mankind, not against it.

If they had seen what we saw, they wouldn't rest until they made sure of it.

Glossary of Important

Japanese

Anami, Korechika, General and Minister of War. For a time the most powerful man in Japan. Stubborn and proud, he was a hard-liner on accepting peace proposals. His loyalty to the Emperor made him keep the Army in line.

Arao, Okisatsu, Colonel. Senior officer of the Military Affairs Section at the War Ministry. Spokesman for the fight-to-the-end group.

Fuha, Hiroshi, Lieutenant Colonel. A staff officer of the Eastern District Army, pupil and friend of General Mori.

Fujimura, Yoshiro, Commander. A naval officer with the Japanese staff in Berlin. Went to Switzerland with the Nazi defeat and became involved with the attempt of German Dr. Hack to get Japan out of the war.

Fujita, Hisanori, Grand Chamberlain. An important member of the Imperial household staff.

Hasunuma, Shigeru, General. The Emperor's chief aide-de-camp.

Hata, Shunroku, Field Marshal. Commander of the Second Army whose headquarters was the target at Hiroshima.

Hatanaka, Kenji, Major. A leader of the no-surrender group, pale, soft-featured, and a pet of General Anami.

Hiranuma, Kiichiro, Baron. Head of the Privy Council. Once an ultra-nationalist who changed with experience, opposed the power of the Kwantung Army and the idea of war with the United States. At the end he teamed with Anami.

Hoshina, Zenshiro, Vice-Admiral. Director of the Bureau of Naval Affairs, Admiral Yonai's assistant.

Ida, Masataka, Lieutenant Colonel. In the Military Affairs Section of the War Ministry. Strong no-surrender man who teamed with Hatanaka.

Inaba, Masao, Lieutenant Colonel. In the Military Affairs Section of the War Ministry. A diehard who professed allegiance to Anami and the Emperor, but worked against their efforts to get troops to surrender.

Ishihara, Sadakichi, Major. A staff officer in the Imperial Guards and a leader of the no-surrender group.

Kawabe, Torashiro, Lieutenant General, Vice Chief of Staff. A diehard until August 14. On hearing of the Emperor's final word, drew up a paper to make sure the Army top brass would cooperate.

Kido, Koichi, Baron. Lord Keeper of the Privy Seal, an old aristocrat, and the closest man to the Emperor.

Koga, Hidemasa, Major. A staff officer of the Imperial Guards, son-in-law of former Premier Tojo. Became a leader in the no-surrender revolt.

Koiso, Kuniaki, General. A compromise Premier after Tojo. Ignored and double-crossed by the military, he finally resigned.

Konoye, Fumimaro, Prince. Aristocrat, three-time Premier, trusted by the Emperor, who worked hard but ineffectively to end the war.

Kozono, Yasuna, Navy Captain. Corps Commander 302d Air Corps, stationed at Atsugi, Japan's largest, best-supplied airbase. A thorough no-surrender type.

Matsumoto, Shunichi. Vice Minister of Foreign Affairs, aide to Foreign Minister Togo.

Mikasa, Prince. Because of his advanced (for the court) social outlook known as the Red Prince. Emperor's youngest brother. Approached by Anami to intercede for the last-ditchers, he scornfully turned the General down.

Mori, Takeshi, Lieutenant General. Head of the First Imperial Guards Division guarding the Emperor and Palace. Trusted by everyone, necessary to the diehards' plot, but too loyal to the Throne.

Okamoto, Suemasa, Foreign Officer. As wartime ambassador to Sweden, he warned Tokyo the United States was having a hard time with its allies about keeping the Emperor.

Onishi, Takijiro, Admiral. Headstrong, arrogant commander, helped draft plan to attack Pearl Harbor, later devised Kamikaze attacks.

Sakomizu, Hisatsune, Chief Secretary to the Cabinet.

Sato, Hiroo, Chief of the War Preparations Section. Not to be confused with Naotake Sato.

Sato, Naotake, unfortunate Japanese ambassador to Moscow.

Shiizaki, Jiro, Lieutenant Colonel. In Military Affairs Section, die-hard friend of Hatanaka.

Sugiyama, Gen, Field Marshal. Chief of Staff at the time of Pearl Harbor. At the request of his government and General Eichelberger, he moved Japanese troops out of the way of American occupation forces, thus avoiding possible clashes.

Suzuki, Kantaro, Baron, Admiral. Last Premier of pre-occupation Japan. Old, deaf, changeable, revered former naval hero, probably senile by war's end, but finally did the job for which he'd been appointed.

Takagi, Sokichi, Admiral. Surveyed course of war for the Navy Ministry. Concluded Japan should sue for peace if Allies took the Solomons, afraid to circulate findings openly, did it quietly, and was ignored.

Takeshita, Masahiko, Lieutenant Colonel. In Military Affairs Section. An intense, emotional diehard and General Anami's brother-in-law.

Tanaka, Seiichi, General. Commander of Eastern District Army, and as such necessary to no-surrender plotters, but he remained loyal to Emperor.

Togo, Shigenori, Diplomat. Foreign Minister at the time of Pearl Harbor and near the end of the war. Brilliant, dogmatic, aloof, acerbic, by 1945, he had become a strong peace-now man.

Tojo, Hideki, General. Premier at the time of Pearl Harbor. Ambitious, narrow-minded product of Kwantung Army, able administrator.

Toyoda, Soemu, Admiral. Navy Chief of Staff. Probably the most brilliant of the three top hard-liners, eloquent xenophobe, excellent in argument. Not to be confused with Admiral Teijiro Toyoda, a member of several cabinets.

Tsukamoto, Makoto, Lieutenant Colonel in the *Kempei Tai*, the military secret police. Intelligent, sophisticated soldier, recalled from Formosa by Colonel Ida to help diehards, but didn't.

Umezu, Yoshijiro, General. Army Chief of Staff. Thorough army man, gruff, rigid, martinet, hard-line fighter to the end for no surrender. Another Kwantung Army product.

Ushijina, Mitsuru, General. Commander in Okinawa, where his tactics were brilliant but unavailing.

Yabe, Kenjiro, Communications. Director of Domestic Branch, NHK, Japan Broadcasting Corporation. Called in to help arrange Emperor's reading rescript to end war.

Yamamoto, Isoruku, Admiral. Navy Commander in Chief. Devised Pearl Harbor strategy as he felt Japan could not defeat United States in a long war, but thought they could neutralize U.S. fleet for a year, which might be enough.

Yonai, Mitsumasa, Admiral. Navy Minister, Premier in 1940. Against alliance with Germany and Italy, critical of war with United States. In retirement 1941–44, brought back to be Navy Minister in Koiso cabinet, continued under old friend Suzuki.

The Big Six: Anami, Suzuki, Togo, Toyoda, Umezu, Yonai.

The *Jushin,* elder statesmen, former premiers: Nabuyoki Abe, Baron Kiichiro Hiranuma, Koki Hirota, Kuniaki Koiso, Prince Fumimaro Konoye, Keisoke Okada, Hideki Tojo, Baron Wakatsuki, Mitzumasa Yonai.

Suzuki's Cabinet, as of June, 1945:

Kantaro Suzuki, Premier
Genki Abe, Home Minister
Tsukizo Akinaga, Director, Overall Planning Board
Korechika Anami, Minister of War
Hosaku Hirose, Finance Minister
Tadaatsu Ishiguro, Minister of Agriculture and Commerce
Naoto Kobiyama, Minister of Transportation
Hiromisa Matsuzako, Minister of Justice
Naoyasu Murase, Director, Legislative Bureau
Kozo Ohta, Education Minister
Tadahiki Okada, Welfare Minister
Hisatsune Sakomizu, Chief Cabinet Secretary
Seizo Sakonji, State Minister
Heigoro Sakurai, State Minister
Hiroshi Shimomura, Director, Information Bureau
Shigenori Togo, Foreign Minister
Teijiro Toyoda, Munitions Minister
Fujihara Yasui, State Minister
Mitsumasa Yonai, Navy Minister

Index

GAVILAN COLLEGE
LIBRARY